Letters to the Churches

By
M. L. Andreasen

TEACH Services, Inc.
P U B L I S H I N G
www.TEACHServices.com • (800) 367-1844

Copyright © 2019 TEACH Services, Inc.
ISBN-13: 978-1-57258-074-9 (Paperback)
ISBN-13: 978-1-4796-1134-8 (ePub)
Library of Congress Control Number: 96-60002

TEACH Services, Inc.
P U B L I S H I N G
www.TEACHServices.com ● (800) 367-1844

Table of Contents

Letter No. 1

THE INCARNATION

Was Christ Exempt?

The word incarnation derives from the two Latin words, *in carnis*, which, together, mean "in flesh" or "in the flesh." As a theological term, it denotes "the taking on of the human form and nature by Jesus, conceived of as the Son of God." In this sense John uses the word when he says, "Hereby know ye the Spirit of God: Every spirit that confesseth that Jesus Christ is come in the flesh is of God: And every spirit that confesseth not that Jesus Christ is come in the flesh is not of God:"…(1 John 4:2, 3). This makes belief in the incarnation a test of disciple-ship, though doubtless more is meant than a mere belief in the histori-cal appearance of Christ.

The coming into the world of a new life—the birth of a babe—is in itself a miracle. Infinitely more so must be the incarnation of the very Son of God. It will ever remain a mystery beyond human comprehension. All man can do is accept it as a part of the plan of redemption which has been gradually revealed since the fall of man in the garden.

For reasons which we cannot fully fathom, God permitted sin. In doing so, however, He also provided a remedy. This remedy comprises the plan of redemption and is bound up with the incarnation, the death, and the resurrection of the Son of God. It cannot be conceived that God did not know what creation would cost Him; and the "council of peace" which decided the matter, must have included provisions for every foreseen contingency. Paul calls this plan "God's wisdom in a mystery, even the wisdom that hath been hidden, which God foreordained before the worlds unto our glory." (1 Corinthians 2:7 A.S.V.).

The phrase "before the worlds" means before there was creation of any kind. Thus the plan of salvation was not an afterthought. It was "foreordained." Even when Lucifer sinned, the plan was not fully revealed, but was "kept in silence through times eternal." (Romans 16:25 A.R.V.) For this, God gives no reason. Paul informs us "that by revelation He (God) made known unto me the mystery…the mystery of Christ which in other ages was not made known unto the sons of men, as it is now revealed unto his holy apostles and prophets by the Spirit." (Ephesians 3:3–5).

BECAME

There are two words in the epistle to the Hebrews which are of interest in this connection. They are "became" in verse ten of chapter two, and "behooved" in verse seventeen of the same chapter.

The Greek word for "became" is *prepo*, and is defined as "suitable," "proper," "fit," "right," "comely." Paul, whom we believe to be the author of Hebrews, is very bold when he thus presumes to attribute motive to God and declares that it is fit and right for God to make Christ "perfect through suffering," (Hebrews 2:10). He considers it "comely" of God to do this; that is, He approves of it. In judging God, he emulates Abraham who was even bolder than Paul. Misunderstanding what God intended to do, Abraham counseled God not to do it. Said he, "Wilt thou also destroy the righteous with the wicked? ...That be far from thee to do after this manner, to slay the righteous with the wicked... That be far from thee: Shall not the judge of all the earth do right?" (Genesis 18:23, 25).

Moses also essayed to admonish God and instruct Him. When Israel danced about the golden calf, God said to Moses, "Let me alone that my wrath may wax hot against them and that I may consume them." (Exodus 32:10). Moses attempted to pacify God and said, "Lord, why doth thy wrath wax hot against thy people? ...Turn from thy fierce wrath and repent of this evil against thy people." (Exodus 32:11, 12). "And the Lord repented of the evil which He thought to do unto His people." (Verse 14).

We readily see that in this interesting episode God was merely testing Abraham, and giving him an opportunity to plead for the people. But we also note that this illustrates God's willingness to talk over matters with His saints; yes, and with those who are not saints. His invitation to mankind is, "Come now, and let us reason together." (Isaiah 1:18). God is anxious to communicate with His people. Neither Abraham nor Moses was rebuked for his boldness.

BEHOOVED

The other word to which we would call attention is "behooved." Speaking of Christ, Paul says, "In all things it behooved him to be made like unto his brethren, that he might be a merciful and faithful high priest in things pertaining to God, to make reconciliation for the sins of the people." (Hebrews 2:17). While "became" in verse 10 is a mild word, "behooved" in verse 17 *(ophilo* in Greek) is a strong word and is defined "under obligation," "ought," "must," "should," "bound," "indebted," "duty," "owe." If Christ is to be a merciful and faithful high priest, Paul says it behooves Him "in all things" to be like His brethren. This is obligatory. It is a duty He owes and must not avoid. He cannot make reconciliation for men unless He takes His place with them and in all things becomes like them. It is not a question of choice. He **should**, He **must**, He **ought** to, He is **under obligation** to, He **owes** it. Unless He has to struggle with the same temptations men do, He cannot sympathize with them. One who has never been hungry, who has never been weak and sick, who has never struggled with temptations, is unable fully to sympathize with those who are thus afflicted.

For this reason it is necessary for Christ **in all things** to become like His brethren. If He is to be touched with the feeling of our infirmities, He must Himself be "compassed with infirmity." (Hebrews 4:15; 5:2). Therefore, if men are afflicted, He also must be afflicted "in all their affliction." (Isaiah 63:9). Christ Himself testifies: "I was not rebellious, neither turned back. I gave my back to the smiters, and my cheeks to them, that plucked off the hair: I hid not my face from shame and spitting." (Isaiah 50:5,6). He "Himself took our infirmities, and bare our sicknesses." (Matthew 8:17). In nothing Christ spared Himself. He did not ask to be exempt from any trial or suffering of man; and God did not exempt Him.

These experiences were all necessary if Christ was to be a merciful high priest. Now, He can sympathize with every child of humanity; for He knows hunger by actual experience and sickness and weakness and temptation and sorrow and affliction and pain and feeling forsaken of God and man. He has been "tempted in all points like as we are, yet without sin." (Hebrews 4:15). It is Christ's partaking of men's afflictions and weaknesses which enables Him to be the sympathizing Saviour that He is.

WAS CHRIST EXEMPT?

With these reflections in mind, we read with astonishment and perplexity, mingled with sorrow, the false statement in *Questions on Doctrine*, p. 383 that Christ was "exempt from the inherited passions and pollutions that corrupt the natural descendants of Adam." To appreciate the import of this assertion, we need to define "exempt" and "passions."

3

The College Standard Dictionary defines exempt: "to free or excuse from some burdensome obligation; free, clear or excuse from some restriction or burden."

New World Dictionary, College Edition, defines exempt: "to take out, deliver, set free as from a rule **which others must observe**; excuse, release…freed from a rule, obligation, etc., **which binds others**; excused, released…exemption implies a release from some obligation or legal requirement, **especially when others are not so released**."

Passion is defined: "originally suffering or agony…any of the emotions as hate, grief, love, fear, joy; the agony and sufferings of Jesus during the crucifixion or during the period following the Last Supper. Passion usually implies a strong emotion that has an overpowering or compelling effect." Passion is an inclusive word. While originally it has reference to sorrow, suffering, agony, it is not confined to these meanings nor to passions of the flesh only, but in-cludes all man's emotions as mentioned above, as well as anger, sor-row, hunger, pity; it includes, in fact, all temptations that incite men to action. To take these emotions away from a man, to exempt him from all temptation, results in a creature less than a man, a kind of no-man, a shadow man, a nonentity, which Markham calls a "brother to the ox." Temptations are the character-building ingredients of life for good or ill, as man reacts to them.

If Christ were exempt from the passions of mankind, He was different from other men, none of whom is so exempt. Such teaching is tragic, and completely contrary to what Seventh-day Adventists have always taught and believed. Christ came as a man among men, asking no favors and receiving no special consideration. According to the terms of the covenant He was not to receive any help from God not available to any other man. This was a necessary condition if His demonstration were to be of any value and His work acceptable. The least deviation from this rule would invalidate the experiment, nullify the agreement, void the covenant, and effectively destroy all hope for man.

Satan's contention has always been that God is unjust in requiring men to keep the law, and doubly unjust in punishing them for not doing what cannot be done, and what no one has ever done. His claim is that God ought at least to make a demonstration to show that it can be done, and done under the same conditions to which men are subject.

Noah, Job, Abraham, David—all were good men, but all failed to come up to God's high standard. "All men have sinned," says Paul. (Romans 3:23).

God was not moved by Satan's challenge; for long before, even from eternity, God had decided upon His course of action. Accordingly, when the time came, God sent "his own son in the likeness of sinful flesh, and for sin, condemned sin in the flesh." (Romans 8:3). Christ did not **condone** sin in the flesh; He **condemned** it, and in so doing upheld the power and authority of the law. By dying on the cross He further enforced the law by paying the penalty required for its transgression, and upheld the infliction of its penalty by paying its demand. He was now in position to forgive without being accused of ignoring the law or setting it aside.

When it became evident that God intended to send His Son and in Him demonstrate that man can keep the law, Satan knew that this would constitute the crisis, and that he must overcome Christ or perish. One thing greatly concerned him. Would Christ come to this earth as a man with the limitations, weaknesses and infirmities which men had brought upon themselves because of excesses? If so, Satan believed he might overcome Him. If God should **exempt** Him from the passions that corrupt the natural descendants of Adam, he could claim that God played favorites, and the test was invalid. In the following quotations we have God's answer:

> "God permitted His Son to come, a helpless babe, subject to the weakness of humanity. He permitted Him to meet life's perils in common with every human soul, to fight the battle as every child of humanity must fight it, at the risk of failure and eternal loss." *The Desire of Ages*, p. 49.

> "Many claim that it was impossible for Christ to be overcome by temptation. Then He could not have been placed in Adam's position...our Saviour took humanity with all its liabilities. He took the nature of man with the possibility of yielding to temptation." *The Desire of Ages,* p. 117.

> "The temptations to which Christ was subject were a terrible reality. As a free agent he was placed on probation with liberty to yield to Satan's temptations and work at cross purposes with God. If this were not so, if it had not been possible for Him to fall, He could not have been tempted in all points as

5

the human family is tempted." *The Youth's Instructor*, Oct. 26,1899.

"When Adam was assailed by the tempter, none of the effects of sin was upon him. He stood in the strength of perfect manhood, possessing the full vigor of mind and body... It was not thus with Jesus when He entered the wilderness to cope with Satan. For four thousand years the race had been decreasing in physical strength, in mental power, in moral worth; and Christ took upon Him the infirmities of degenerate humanity. **Only thus** could He rescue man from the lowest depth of his degradation." *The Desire of Ages*, p. 117.

Christ "vanquished Satan in the same nature over which Satan obtained the victory. The enemy was overcome by Christ in His human nature. The power of the Saviour's Godhead was hidden. He overcame in human nature relying upon God for power. This is the privilege of all." *The Youth's Instructor*, April 25, 1901.

"Letters have been coming in to me, **affirming that Christ could not have had the same nature as man, for if He had, He would have fallen under similar temptations. If He did not have man's nature, He could not be our example. If He was not a partaker of our nature, He could not have been tempted as man has been. If it were not possible for Him to yield to temptations,** He could not be our Helper. It was a solemn reality that Christ came to fight the battle as man, in man's behalf. His temptation and victory tell us that humanity must copy the Pattern; men must become a partaker of the divine nature." *Review and Herald*, February 18, 1890.

"Christ bore the sins and infirmities of the race as they existed when He came to the earth to help man.... He took human nature, and bore the infirmities of the degenerate race." *The Temptations of Christ*, pp. 30, 31.

If Christ had been exempt from passions, He would have been unable to understand or help mankind. It, therefore, behooved Him "in all things to be made like unto his brethren, that he might be a merciful and faithful high priest...for in that he himself hath suffered, being tempted, he is able to succor them that are tempted." (Hebrews 2:17, 18). A Saviour who has never been tempted, never has had to battle with passions, who has never "offered up prayers and supplications with strong crying and tears unto him who was able to save him from death," who "though he were a son" never learned obedience by the things He suffered, but was "exempt" from the very things that a true Saviour must experience: such a savior is what this new theology offers us. It is not the kind of Savior I need, nor the world. One who has never struggled with passions can have no understanding of their power, nor has he ever had the joy of overcoming them. If God extended special favors and exemptions to Christ, in that very act He disqualified Him for His work. There can be no heresy more harmful than that here discussed. It takes away the Saviour I have known and substitutes for Him a weak personality, not considered by God capable of resisting and conquering the passions which He asks men to overcome.

It is, of course, patent to all, that no one can claim to believe the *Testimonies* and also believe in the new theology that Christ was exempt from human passions. It is one thing or the other. The denomination is now called upon to decide. To accept the teaching of *Questions on Doctrine* necessitates giving up faith in the Gift God has given this people.

SOME HISTORY

It may interest the reader to know how these new doctrines came to be accepted by the leaders, and how they came to be included in *Questions on Doctrine*, and thus receive official standing.

The question of the nature of Christ while in the flesh is one of the foundation pillars of Christianity. On this doctrine hangs the salvation of man. The apostle John makes it a deciding factor by saying, "Every spirit that confesseth that Jesus Christ is come in the flesh, is of God: And every spirit that confesseth not that Jesus Christ is come in the flesh, is not of God." (1 John 4:2, 3).

In what kind of flesh did Jesus come to this earth? We repeat a quotation which we have given above: "Christ took upon Him the infirmities of degenerate humanity. Only thus could He rescue man from the lowest depth of his degradation." *The Desire of Ages*, p. 117.

Only as Christ placed Himself on the level of the humanity He had come to save, could He demonstrate to men how to overcome their infirmities and passions. If the men with whom He associated had understood that He was **exempt** from the passions with which they had to battle, His influence would immediately have been destroyed and He would be reckoned a deceiver. His pronouncement, "I have overcome the world," (John 16:33) would be accepted as a dishonest boast; for without passions He had nothing to overcome. His promise that "to him that overcometh will I grant to sit with me in my throne, even as **I also overcame** and am set down with my Father in his throne," (Revelation 3:21) would be met by the claim that if God would **exempt them** from passions, they also could do what Christ had done.

That God exempted Christ from the passions that corrupt men, is the acme of all heresy. It is destruction of all true religion and completely nullifies the plan of redemption, and makes God a deceiver and Christ His accomplice. Great responsibility rests upon those who teach such false doctrine to the destruction of souls. The truth, of course, is that God "spared not his own Son, but delivered him up for us" (Romans 8:32); rather, because His nature was sensitive to the least slight or disrespect or contempt, His tests were harder and His temptations stronger than any we have to endure. He resisted "even unto blood." No, God did not spare or exempt Him. In His agony He "offered up prayers and supplications with strong crying and tears unto Him that was able to save Him from death, and was heard in that he feared." (Hebrews 5:7). "Though he were a son, yet learned he obedience by the things which he suffered." (Verse 8).

In view of all this, we repeat the question, how did this God-dishonoring doctrine find its way into this denomination? Was it the result of close and prayerful study by competent men over a series of years, and were the final conclusions submitted to the denomination in public representative meetings, advertised beforehand in the *Review and Herald* giving the details of what changes were contemplated, as the denomination has voted as the proper procedure? None of these things were done. An anonymous book appeared, and men were judged and the brakes tightened on anyone who objected.

Here is the story of how these new doctrines found their way into the denomination as reported by Dr. Donald Grey Barnhouse, editor of the religious journal, *Eternity*, in the September, 1956, issue of his magazine, later issued as a copyrighted article entitled "Are Seventh-day Adventists Christians?" With permission we quote from this article. We may inject that Dr. Barnhouse advises us that the entire

8

content of the article was submitted to the Adventist brethren for approval before publication. The fact that this report has been in print for nearly three years and no correction or protest has been forthcoming from our leaders would strongly argue that they accept the truthfulness of the account.

Dr. Barnhouse reports that "a little less than two years ago it was decided that Mr. Martin should undertake research in connection with Seventh-day Adventism." Mr. Walter R. Martin was at that time a candidate for degree of Doctor of Philosophy in New York University and also connected with the editorial staff of *Eternity*. Wishing to get firsthand and reliable information, Mr. Martin went to Washington to the Adventist headquarters where he got in touch with some of the leaders. "The response was immediate and enthusiastic." Mr. Martin "immediately...perceived that the Adventists were strenuously denying certain doctrinal positions which had been previously attributed to them. Chief among these were the question of the mark of the beast, and the nature of Christ while in the flesh." Mr. Martin "pointed out to them that in their bookstore adjoining the building in which these meetings were taking place, a certain volume published by them and written by one of their ministers categorically stated the contrary to what they were now asserting. The leaders sent for the book, discovered that Mr. Martin was correct, and immediately brought this fact to the attention of the General Conference officers, that the situation might be remedied and such publications be corrected."

This concerned particularly the doctrine of the mark of the beast, one of the fundamental doctrines of the Adventist church held from near its beginning. When the leaders discovered that Mr. Martin was correct, they suggested to the officers that the situation be "remedied and such publications be corrected." This was done. We are not informed which publications were so "remedied and corrected," nor if the authors were notified before the changes were made; nor if the duly appointed book committee was consulted; nor if the book editors or the publishing house were agreeable to the changes. We do know, however, that in the Sabbath School Lessons for the second quarter of 1958, which dealt with the book of Revelation, chapter by chapter, the thirteenth chapter which discusses the mark of the beast was entirely omitted. Chapter 12 was there, so was chapter 14, but there was no chapter 13. The Sabbath School Lessons had evidently been "remedied and corrected."

It is certainly anomalous when a minister of another denomination has enough influence with our leaders to have them correct our theology, effect a change in the teaching of the denomination on a most vital doctrine of the church, and even invade the Sabbath Schools of the world and withhold from them the important lessons of Revelation 13. For our leaders to accept this is tantamount to an abdication of their leadership.

THE SAME PROCEDURE

But this is not all. Dr. Barnhouse reports that the same procedure was repeated regarding the nature of Christ while in the flesh, the subject with which we have been here dealing. Our leaders assured Mr. Martin that "the majority of the denomination has always held (the nature of Christ while in the flesh) to be sinless, holy, and perfect, despite the fact certain of their writers have occasionally gotten into print with contrary views completely repugnant to the church at large."

If our leaders told Martin this, they told the greatest untruth ever. For the denomination has never held any other view than that expressed by Mrs. White in the quotations used in this article. We challenge our leaders, or anybody, to produce proof of their assertion. How grossly untrue is the statement that certain writers got into print with views "completely repugnant to the church at large." Mrs. White was one of those writers who "got into print." Hear also what our standard book, *Bible Readings for the Home Circle*, sold to the public by the millions, has to say on the subject. I have before me two copies, one printed by the Pacific Press in 1916, the other by the Southern Publishing house in 1944. They both read alike. Here is the accepted teaching by the denomination:

> "In His humanity Christ partook of our sinful, fallen nature. If not, then, He was not made 'like unto His brethren,' was not 'in all points tempted like as we are,' did not overcome as we have to overcome, and is not, therefore, the complete and perfect Saviour man needs and must have to be saved. The idea that Christ was born of an immaculate or sinless mother (Protestants do not claim this for the virgin Mary), inherited no tendencies to sin, and for this reason did not sin, removes Him from the realm of a fallen world, and from the very place where help is needed. On His human side, Christ

inherited just what every child of Adam inherits, a sinful, fallen nature. On the divine side, from His very conception He was begotten and born of the Spirit. And this was done to place mankind on vantage-ground, and to demonstrate that in the same way every one who is 'born of the Spirit' may gain like victories over sin in his own sinful flesh. Thus each one is to overcome as Christ overcame (Revelation 3:21). Without this birth there can be no victory over temptation, and no salvation from sin (John 3:3–7)." Page 21.

In explanation of how these writers "got into print" with their views, our leaders told Mr. Martin that "they had among their number certain members of their 'lunatic fringe,' even as there are similar **wild-eyed irresponsibles** in every field of fundamental Christianity." I think this is going too far. Mrs. White did not belong to the "lunatic fringe" who got into print, nor did the authors of *Bible Readings*. Our leaders should make a most humble apology to the denomination for such a slur upon their members. It is almost unbelievable that they should ever have made such statements. But the accusation has been in print nearly three years, and there has been no protest of any kind. I am humiliated that such accusations should have been made, and even more so that our leaders are completely callous in their attitude toward them.

That the reader may see for himself the original report of Dr. Barnhouse, I append a copy of the reprint, "Are Seventh-day Adventists Christians?" This is not the report in full, but only that part which relates to the questions here discussed. Later I shall present other extracts.

"A little less than two years ago it was decided that Mr. Martin should undertake research in connection with Seventh-day Adventism. We got into touch with the Adventists saying that we wished to treat them fairly and would appreciate the opportunity of interviewing some of their leaders. The response was immediate and enthusiastic.

"Mr. Martin went to Takoma Park, Washington, D.C., the headquarters of the Seventh-day Adventist movement. At first the two groups looked upon each other with great suspicion. Mr. Martin had read a vast quantity of Adventist literature and presented them with a series of approximately forty questions concerning their theological position. On a second visit he was presented with scores of pages of detailed theological answers to his questions. Immediately it was perceived that the Adventists were strenuously denying certain doctrinal positions which have been previously attributed to them. As Mr. Martin read their answers he came, for example, upon a statement that they repudiated absolutely the thought that Seventh-day Sabbath keeping was a basis for salvation and a denial of any teaching that the keeping of the first day of the week is as yet considered to be the receiving of the anti-Christian 'mark of the beast.' He pointed out to them that in their book store adjoining the building, in which these meetings were taking place a certain volume published by them and written by one of their ministers categorically stated the contrary to what they were now asserting. The leaders sent for the book, discovered that Mr. Martin was correct, and immediately brought this fact to the attention of the General Conference Officers, that this situation might be remedied and such publications be corrected. This same procedure was repeated regarding the nature of Christ while in the flesh which the majority of the denomination has always held to be sinless, holy, and perfect despite the fact that certain of their writers have occasionally gotten into print with contrary views completely repugnant to the Church at large. They further explained to Mr. Martin that they had among their number certain members of their 'lunatic fringe' even as there are similar wild-eyed irresponsibles in every field of fundamental Christianity. This action of the Seventh-day Adventists was indicative of similar steps that were taken subsequently.

"Mr. Martin's book on Seventh-day Adventism will appear in print within a few months. It will carry a foreword by responsible leaders of the Seventh-day Adventist church to the effect that they have not been misquoted in the volume and that the areas of agreement and disagreement as set forth by Mr. Martin are accurate from their point of view as well as from our evangelical point of view. All of Mr. Martin's references to a new Adventist volume on their doctrines will be from the page proof of their book, which will appear in print simultaneously with his work. Henceforth any fair criticism of the Adventist movement must refer to these simultaneous publications.

"The position of the Adventists seems to some of us in certain cases to be a new position; to them it may be merely the position of the majority group of sane leadership which is determined to put the brakes on any members who seek to hold views divergent from that of the responsible leadership of the denomination.

"To avoid charges that have been brought against them by evangelicals, Adventists have already worked out arrangements that the *Voice of Prophecy* radio program and the *Signs of the Times*, their largest paper, be identified as presentations of the Seventh-day Adventist church."

In closing this paper, I wish to re-emphasize certain salient facts:

1. *Questions on Doctrine*, page 383, states that Christ was exempt. The Spirit of Prophecy makes clear that Christ was **not exempt** from the temptations and passions that afflict men. Whoever accepts the new theology must reject the *Testimonies*. There is no other choice.

2. Mr. Martin was instrumental in having our teaching on the **mark of the beast** and the **nature of Christ in the flesh** changed. Similar changes were made in other books, but we are not informed what those changes are.

3. Our leaders have promised not to proselytize. This effectively will stop our work for the world. And we have promised to report to Mr. Martin those who transgress.

4. We have been threatened to have **the brakes applied** to such as fail to believe and follow the leaders. Such are characterized as **"wild-eyed irresponsibles"** and are said to constitute the **"lunatic fringe."**

5. We are appalled to learn that in some way these evangelical clergymen have had enough influence with our leaders to cause the *Voice of Prophecy* and the *Signs of the Times* to trim their sails to "avoid charges that have been brought against them by evangelicals." This is terrifying news. These organs are instruments of God, and it is unbelievable that the leaders should permit any outside influence to affect them. In this a great sin against the denomination has been committed that can be blotted out only by deep repentance of the guilty parties, or in lieu of this, that the men concerned quietly resign from holy office.

Our members are largely unaware of the conditions existing, and every effort is being made to keep them in ignorance. Orders have been issued to keep everything secret, and it will be noted that even at the late General Conference session no report was given of our leaders' trafficking with the evangelicals and making alliances with them. Our officials are playing with fire, and the resulting conflagration will fulfill the prediction that the coming Omega "will be of a most startling nature."

Seven times I have asked for a hearing, and I have been promised one, but only on the condition that I meet privately with certain men, and that no record be given me of the proceedings. I have asked for a public hearing, or if it is to be a private one, that a tape recording be made, and that I be given a copy. This has been denied me. As I cannot have such a hearing, I am writing these messages which contain, and will contain, what I would have said at such a hearing. Can the reader surmise the reason why the officers do not want the hearing I ask?

I am a Seventh-day Adventist, and I love this message that I have preached for so long. I grieve deeply as I see the foundation pillars being destroyed, the blessed truths that have made us what we are abandoned.

The next letter will be sent only to those who order it, so send name and address. Extra copies of this or subsequent letters may be had at ten cents each.

I am thankful to be in good health and wish the blessing of the Lord may be with each reader. We have come to strenuous times, and it behooves each to keep close to God in these perilous times. The Lord be with you.

Letter No. 2
ATTEMPTED TAMPERING

Early in the summer of 1957 I had placed in my hands, providentially I believe, a copy of the minutes of the White Board of Trustees for May of that year. For those who are not familiar with this board, I may state that it is a small committee appointed to have in trust the large volume of letters, manuscripts, and books left by the late Mrs. E. G. White. In counsel with the officers of the denomination, the board decides who is to have access to the material, and to what extent and for what purpose; what is to be published and what is not; and what material is not to be made available at all.

Much of the work of the committee consists in examining and editing these writings and recommending for publication such matter as appears to be of permanent value. This work is of great importance to the church, for only that which is released by the board sees the light of day. During her lifetime Mrs. White herself did much of the work of selecting and editing, and in all cases she had the oversight of what was done. All knew that whatever was published was under her supervision and that it had her approval. The board now has taken over this work.[1]

TWO MEN AND THE COMMITTEE

According to the White minutes, it was on the first day of May 1957, that two men, members of the committee which had been appointed to write the book that came to be known as *Questions on Doctrine*, were invited by the board to meet with them to discuss a question that had received some consideration at a meeting the previous January. It concerned statements made by Mrs. White in regard to the atonement now in progress in the sanctuary above. This conception did not agree with the conclusions reached by the leaders of the

---

1   From E. G. White Estates, Inc., March 1996: "Andreasen refers to policies that formerly pertained to unpublished materials left in the custody of the Trustees by Ellen G. White. Under current policies, all of Ellen G. White's writings are available for study."

denomination in counsel with the evangelicals. To understand this fully, and its importance, it is necessary to review some history.

The Adventist leaders had for some time been in contact with two ministers of another faith, evangelicals, Dr. Barnhouse and Mr. Martin, respectively editor and an assistant editor of the religious journal *Eternity*, published in Philadelphia, and had discussed with them various of our doctrines. In these conversations, as in the numerous letters that passed between them, the evangelicals had raised serious objections to some of our beliefs. The question of greatest importance was whether Adventists could be considered Christians while holding such views as the doctrine of the sanctuary; the 2300 days; the date 1844; the investigative judgment; and Christ's atoning work in the sanctuary in Heaven since 1844. Our men expressed the desire that the Adventist church be reckoned as one of the regular Protestant churches, a Christian church, not a sect.

The two groups spent "hundreds of hours" studying, and wrote many hundreds of pages. The evangelicals visited our headquarters in Takoma Park, and our men visited Philadelphia and were guests of Dr. Barnhouse in his comfortable home. From time to time other men were called into consultation on such matters as the *Voice of Prophecy* and our periodicals, all with a view of ascertaining what stood in the way of our being recognized as a Christian denomination.

After long and protracted discussions, the two parties came at last to a working agreement, and though the evangelicals still objected to a number of our doctrines, they were willing to recognize us as Christians. We would need to make some changes in some of our books in regard to the "mark of beast" and, also, "regarding the nature of Christ while in the flesh." *Eternity*, September, 1956. This was brought to the "attention of the General Conference officers, that the situation might be remedied and **such publications might be corrected**." The corrections were made, and "this action of the Seventh-day Adventists was indicative of **similar steps that were taken subsequently**." *Ibid.* We are not informed what other books were "remedied and corrected." The evangelicals published a report of their conferences with the Adventists in *Eternity* from which the above quotations are taken. Dr. Barnhouse states that they took the precaution to submit their manuscript to the Adventists so that no misstatement or error might occur. The Adventists published no report. Even at the General Conference session last year, the matter was not discussed. Only a few knew that there had been any conferences with the evangelicals. There were rumors that the Adventist leaders had been in conference with the evangelicals, but that was considered by some only as hearsay. The few who did know, kept their counsel. There seemed to be a conspiracy of secrecy.

Till this day we do not know, and are not supposed to know, who carried on the conferences with the evangelicals. We do not know, and are not supposed to know, who wrote *Questions on Doctrine*. Diligent inquiry produced no result. We do not know, and are not supposed to know, just what changes were made, and in what books, concerning the mark of the beast and the nature of Christ while in the flesh. We do not know who authorized the omission of the thirteenth chapter [in Revelation] in our Sabbath School Lessons for the second quarter of 1958, which deals with the mark of the beast. Dr. Barnhouse reports that to "avoid charges brought against them by the evangelicals," the Adventists "worked out arrangements" that concerned the *Voice of Prophecy* and the *Signs of the Times*. What was "worked out" we do not know and are not told. Should we not have a detailed report? We, of course, also wonder how it came to pass that ministers of another denomination had any voice or any say whatsoever in how we conduct our work. Have our leaders abdicated? How is it that they consult the evangelicals and keep our own people in the dark?

WHAT WAS DONE AT THE CONFERENCES?

For a report of this we are confined almost entirely to the published account in *Eternity*.

The subject that took up much of the time at the conferences was that of the sanctuary. Dr. Barnhouse was frank in his estimate of this doctrine. In particular did he object to our teaching on the investigative judgment which he characterized as "the most colossal, psychological, face-saving phenomenon in religious history." Later he called it "the unimportant and almost naive doctrine of the 'investigative judgment,'" and said that "any effort to establish it is **stale, flat, and unprofitable**." *Eternity*, September, 1956.

Dr. Barnhouse, in discussing Hiram Edson's explanation of the disappointment in 1844 says that the assumption that Christ

"had a work to perform in the most holy before coming to this earth...is a human, face-saving idea (which) some uninformed Adventists...carried to fantastic, literalistic extremes.

Mr. Martin and I heard the Adventist leaders say, flatly, that they repudiated all such extremes. This they said in no uncertain terms. Further, they do not believe, as some of their earlier teachers taught that Jesus' atoning work was not completed on Calvary, but instead that He was still carrying on a second ministerial work since 1844. This idea is also totally repudiated."

Note these statements: The idea that Christ "had a work to perform in the most holy place before coming to this earth...is a human, face-saving idea," "Mr. Martin and I heard the Adventist leaders say flatly that they repudiated such extremes. This they said in no uncertain terms."

I think it is due the denomination to have a clear-cut statement from our leaders if Dr. Barnhouse and Mr. Martin told the truth when they heard our leaders say that they repudiated the idea that Christ had a work to do in the second apartment before coming to this earth. This question demands a clear-cut answer.

ATTEMPTED TAMPERING

Before reporting further what was done at the conferences let us come back to the two men who on that first day of May, 1957, met with the White Board of Trustees to seek their counsel and, also, to make a suggestion. The men were well acquainted with the statements made by Dr. Barnhouse and Mr. Martin, that the idea of Christ's ministry in the second apartment in the sanctuary had been totally repudiated. This had been in print several months at that time, and had not been protested. The men, however, did not need the printed statement, for both of them had had a part in the discussions with the evangelicals. One of them in particular had taken a prominent part in the conferences, had visited Dr. Barnhouse in his home, had spoken in Dr. Barnhouse's churches at his invitation. He was one of the four men who really carried the load, and the one chosen to accompany Mr. Martin on his tour of the west coast to speak in our churches. He was held in high esteem by Dr. Barnhouse. This feeling was mutual.

About the time when the two men first visited the vault, a series of articles appeared in the *Ministry* which claimed to be "the Adventist understanding of the atonement, confirmed and illuminated and clarified by the Spirit of Prophecy." In the February issue, 1957, the statement occurs that the "sacrificial act on the cross (is a complete,

18

perfect, and final atonement for man's sin." This pronouncement is in harmony with the belief of our leaders, as Dr. Barnhouse quoted them. It is also in harmony with a statement signed by a chief officer in a personal letter: "You cannot, Brother Andreasen, take away from us this precious teaching that Jesus made a complete and all-sufficient atoning sacrifice on the cross. ...This we shall ever hold fast, and continue to proclaim it, even as our **dear venerated forefathers in the faith."**

It would be interesting if the writer would produce proof of his assertion. The truth is, our forefathers believed and proclaimed no such thing. They did not believe that the work on the cross was complete and all-sufficient. They did believe that a ransom was there paid and that **this** was all-sufficient; but the final atonement awaited Christ's entrance into the most holy in 1844. This the Adventists have always taught and believed, and this is the old and established doctrine which our venerated forefathers believed and proclaimed. They could not teach that the **atonement** on the cross was **final, complete** and **all sufficient**, and yet believe that another atonement, also final, occurred in 1844. Such would be absurd and meaningless. Paying the penalty for our sin was, indeed, a vital and necessary part of God's plan for our salvation, but it was by no means all. It was, as it were, placing in the bank of Heaven a sum sufficient and in every way adequate for any contingency, and which could be drawn on by and for each individual as needed. This payment was "the precious blood of Christ, as of a lamb, without blemish and without spot." (1 Peter 1:19). In His death on the cross Jesus "paid it all;" but the precious treasure becomes efficacious for us only as Christ draws upon it for us, and this must await the coming into the world of each individual; hence, the atonement must continue as long as people are born. Hear this:

> "There is an inexhaustible fund of perfect obedience accruing from His obedience. How is it, that such an infinite treasure is not appropriated? In Heaven, the merits of Christ, His self-denial and self-sacrifice, are treasured up as incense, to be offered up with the prayers of His people." *General Conference Bulletin,* Vol. 3, pp. 101, 102, Fourth Quarter, 1899.

Note the phrases; "inexhaustible fund," "infinite treasure," "merits of Christ." This fund was deposited at the cross, but not "used up" there. It is "treasured up" and offered up with the prayers of God's people. And especially since 1844 is this fund drawn on heavily as

God's people advance to holiness; but it is not exhausted, there is sufficient and to spare. Hear again:

> "He who through His own atonement provided for them an **infinite fund** of moral power will not fail to employ this power in their behalf. He will impute to them His own righteousness... There is an **inexhaustible fund** of perfect obedience accruing from His obedience...as sincere, humble prayers ascend to the throne of God, Christ mingles with them the merits of His own life of perfect obedience. Our prayers are made fragrant by this incense. Christ has pledged Himself to intercede in our behalf, and the Father always hears His Son." *Ibid.*

When we pray, in this very year of 1959, Christ intercedes for us and mingles with our prayers "the merits of His own life of perfect obedience. Our prayers are made fragrant by this incense...and the Father always hears His Son."

Contrast this with the statement in *Questions on Doctrine*, page 381: "(Jesus) appeared in the presence of God for us... But it was not with the **hope** of obtaining something for us at that time or at some future time. No! **He had already obtained it for us on the cross.**" [Emphasis his.] Note the picture: Christ appears in the presence of God **for us**. He pleads, but He gets nothing. For 1800 years He pleads, and gets nothing. Does He not know that He already has it? Will no one inform Him that it is useless to plead? He Himself has "no hope" of getting anything now or at any future time. And yet He pleads, and keeps on pleading. What a sight for the angels! And this is represented to be Adventist teaching! This is the book that has the approval of Adventist leaders and is sent out to the world to show what we believe. May God forgive us. How can we stand before the world and convince any one that we believe in a Saviour who is mighty to save, when we present Him as pleading in vain before the Father?

But thank God, this is not Adventist doctrine. Hear this from Sister White, as quoted above: "Christ has pledged Himself to intercede in our behalf, and **the Father always hears His Son.**" This is Christianity, and the other **is not**.

Shall we remain **silent** under such conditions? Says Sister White:

"For the past fifty years every phase of heresy has been brought to bear upon us...especially concerning the ministration of Christ in the Heavenly sanctuary... Do you wonder that when I see the beginning of a work that would re-move some of the pillars of our faith, I have something to say? I must obey the command, 'Meet it!'" Series B, No. 2, p. 58.

Again: "The enemy of souls has sought to bring in the supposition that a great reformation was to take place among Seventh-day Adventists, and that this reformation would consist in giving up doctrines which stand as the pillars of our faith, and engaging in a process of reorganization. Were this reformation to take place, what would result? The principles of truth that God in His wisdom has given to the remnant church, would be discarded. The fundamental truths that have sustained the work for the last fifty years, would be accounted as error. A new organization would be established. Books of a new order would be written. A system of intellectual philosophy would be introduced... Nothing would be allowed to stand in the way of the new movement." *Ibid,* pp. 54, 55.

"Shall we keep silent for fear of hurting their feelings?...Shall we keep silent for fear of injuring their influence, while souls are being beguiled... My message is: No longer consent to listen without protest to the perversion of truth." *Ibid.* pp. 9,15 [Emphasis original publisher.]

THE MAY 1st MEETING

I doubt that the Adventist leaders were fully aware of the many references in Mrs. White's works to the atonement now in progress in the heavenly sanctuary since 1844. If they were, how would they have dared to take the position they did in regard to the sanctuary question?This idea finds support in the apparent surprise of the two men who visited the vault and stated that in their research they had "become acutely aware of the E. G. White statements which indicate that the atoning work of Christ is now in progress in the heavenly sanctuary." *Minutes,* May 1, 1957, page 1483. Why did they become acutely aware? The discovery seemed to surprise them. In using the plural, statements, they admit of more than one reference. I do not know how many they found. I

21

have found seventeen, and there are doubtless others. And why did they use the word "indicate?" Sister White does more than indicate. She makes definite pronouncements. Here are some of them:

"At the termination of the 2300 days, in 1844, Christ entered the most holy place of the heavenly sanctuary, to perform the closing work of atonement, preparatory to His coming." *Great Controversy*, p. 422.

"Christ had only completed one part of His work as our Intercessor to enter upon another portion of the work, and He still pleaded His blood before the Father in behalf of sinners." *Ibid*, 429. At "the opening of the most holy place of the heavenly sanctuary, in **1844 (as) Christ entered there to perform the closing work of the atonement**. They saw that He was now officiating before the ark of God, pleading His blood in behalf of sinners. *Ibid*, p 433.

"Christ is represented as **continually** standing at the altar, momentarily offering up the sacrifice for the sins of the world. ...A Mediator is essential because of the continual commission of sin. ...Jesus presents the oblation offered **for every offense** and every shortcoming of the sinner." *MS*. 50, 1900.

These statements are definite. It was at the end of the 2300 days, in 1844, that Christ entered the most holy "to perform the closing work of the atonement." "He had ONLY COMPLETED ONE PART OF HIS WORK as our intercessor," in the first apartment. Now He "enters upon another portion of the work." He pleads "His blood before the Father." He is "continually standing at the altar." This is necessary "because of the continual commission of sin." "Jesus presents the oblation for every offense and every shortcoming of the sinner. This argues a **continuing, present atonement**. He offers up "momentarily." "Jesus presents the oblation offered for every offense." "He ever liveth to make intercession for them." (Hebrews 7:25).

It is presumed that when the two men stated that they had "become acutely aware of the E. G. White statements which indicate that the atoning work of Christ is now in progress in the heavenly sanctuary," that they had read the quotations here given and perhaps others. In view of this knowledge, what did they suggest should be done? Would they change their former erroneous opinions and harmonize with the plain words of the Spirit of Prophecy? No, on the contrary, they "suggested to the trustees that some footnotes or Appendix notes might appear in certain of the E. G. White books clarifying very largely in the words of Ellen White **our** understanding of the various phases of the atoning work of Christ." *Minutes*, p. 1483.

Ponder this amazing statement. They admit that Sister White says that "the atoning work of Christ is now in progress in the heavenly sanctuary," and then they propose that insertions be made in some of Sister White's books that will give **our** understanding of the atonement! They were, however, only acting in harmony with the official statement in *Questions on Doctrine* that when one reads "in the writings of Ellen G. White that Christ is making atonement now, it should be understood that we simply mean that Christ is now making application" etc., page 354, 355.

If Sister White were now living and should read this, she would most certainly deal with presumptuous writers and in words that could be understood. She would not concede the right of anyone, whoever he might be, to change what she has written or interpret it so as to vitiate its clear meaning. The claim which *Questions on Doctrine* makes that she means what she does not say, effectively destroys the force of all she has ever written. If we have to consult an inspired interpreter from Washington before knowing what she means, we might better discard the *Testimonies* altogether. May God save His people.

Early in this century when the fate of the denomination hung in the balance, Sister White wrote: "Satan has laid his plans to undermine our faith in the history of the cause and work of God. I am deeply in earnest as I write this: Satan is working with **men in prominent position** to sweep away the foundations of our faith. Shall we allow this to be done, brethren?" *Review and Herald*, Nov. 12, 1903.

Answering her question, "shall we allow this to be done?" she says:

"My message is: No longer consent without protest to the perversion of truth... I have been instructed to warn our people; for many are in danger of receiving theories and sophistries that undermine the foundation pillars of the faith." *Letters to Physicians and Ministers, Series B, No. 2,* p. 15. "For the past fifty years every phase of heresy has been brought to bear upon us, to becloud our minds regarding the teaching of the Word—**especially concerning the ministration of Christ in the heavenly sanctuary**. ...But the way-marks which have made us what we are, **are to be preserved, and they will be preserved**, as God has signified through His Word and the testimony of His Spirit. He calls upon us to hold firmly, with the grip of faith to the fundamental principles that are based upon unquestionable authority." Ibid. p. 59. "Do you wonder that when I see the beginning of a work that would remove some of the pillars of our faith, I have something to say? *I must obey the command, 'Meet it,.'* " *Ibid,* page 58. [Emphasis supplied.]

COME PROMINENTLY TO THE FRONT

After the two men had suggested the insertion of notes and explanations in some of the E. G. White books that would give the reader the impression that she was not opposed to their new interpretation, they had another suggestion to make. "This is a matter," they said, "which will come prominently to the front in the near future, and (that) we would do well to move forward with the preparation and inclusion of such notes in future printings of the E. G. White books." *Minutes*, p. 1483.

I leave to the reader to decide why the men were in haste to get the notes and explanations into the Ellen White books. Could it be that doing this would constitute a *"fait accompli,"* an accomplished fact, a thing that had already been done and which would be difficult or impossible to change? This is an important consideration, for there is reason to believe that things are happening to other of our books, and there is a definite movement to change our doctrine in other matters. This should be further explored, before it is too late.

May 2 this is recorded in the *Minutes:* **E. G. White Statements on the Atoning Work of Christ**—"The meeting of the Trustees held May 1 closed with no action taken on the question which was discussed at length—suitable footnotes or explanations regarding the E. G. White statements on the atoning work of Christ, which indicate a continuing work at the present time in Heaven. Inasmuch as the chairman of our board will be away from Washington for the next four months, and the involvements in this question are such that it must have the most careful consideration and counsel, it was

"VOTED, That we defer consideration until a later time of the matters that were brought to our attention by Elders "x" and "y" involving the E. G. White statements concerning *the continuing* atoning *work of Christ." Minutes of the White Board*, p. 1488.

It was presumably four months later when Elder Olson had returned that a vote was taken not to grant the request. This was eight months after their first January meeting, by which time the matter had been exposed.

CORRESPONDENCE WITH WASHINGTON

After this situation came to my knowledge, I did a deal of praying. What was my responsibility in this matter, or did I have any? I confided to no one. I decided my first responsibility would be to the officials in Washington, so I wrote to headquarters. I was there informed that I had no right to the information I had. That was supposed to be secret, and I had no right even to read the documents.

After four letters were passed, I was told that they did not care to discuss the matter further. The matter was settled. When I inquired if this meant that the door was closed, I received the reply: "I have considered the matter to which you have referred as closed." As to the scurrilous and untrue article in the *Ministry*, "I have discussed this with the brethren concerned and would like to leave the matter there." So the door was closed.

Here are some of the official pronouncements: "**The minutes are confidential and not intended for public use**. If wrong is committed, is it forbidden to expose it merely because some want to keep it confidential?

"**You are doing this upon hearsay and upon confidential minutes which you had no right even to read.**" No one ever talked to me of this or informed me. I read the minutes and acted upon them. The minutes are not hearsay. They are officially documented and signed.

"**...you have no right even to read.**" When I have evidence that to me seems destructive of the faith, am I to close my eyes to what I consider premeditated attempts to mislead the people by the insertions of notes, explanations, and appendix notes in the books of Mrs. White? Is this officially approved?

"I wish to repeat what I wrote before, that men have a perfect right to go to boards, including the White Estate group, and make their suggestions without fear of being disciplined or dealt with as heretics."

This was re-emphasized: **"I reaffirm my former statement that I believe these brethren were entirely in order in going to the properly delegated and responsible individuals with any suggestion they had for study."**

This makes it clear that the act of the two brethren is officially approved; that they did not do anything for which they should be reproved, but that they did what they had a perfect right to do. I do not think our people will welcome this new principle.

"To suggest that good and faithful Seventh-day Adventist men sat down to tamper with the pillars of our faith is as far from fact as the poles are apart:...tampering with the *Testimonies*, when no such thing ever took place, nor was there any attempt ever made to do this,"

I leave to the reader's decision just why the men went to the committee: did they not come to have insertions, notes, Appendix notes, explanations made in "some of the E. G. White books"? While the committee eventually decided not to do this, the guilt of the men is not changed by that fact. To assert that as for "tampering with the *Testimonies* (when) no such thing ever took place nor was there any attempt ever made to do this," the *Minutes* speak for themselves.

A SERIOUS SITUATION

This vault episode brings into focus a serious situation. It is not merely a matter of two men attempting to have insertions made in some of Mrs. White's books. A much more serious thing is that this act had the approval of the administration, who stated that the men had a "perfect right" to do what they did. This pronouncement opens the way for others to follow, and as the matter is kept secret, great abuse could readily result. Undoubtedly, if the matter is left to a vote of the people, there will be no permission for any to tamper, or attempt to tamper, with the writings of Ellen G. White.

The men who visited the vault May 1, as related, stated clearly that they had discovered that Mrs. White taught plainly "that the atoning work of Christ is now in progress in the heavenly sanctuary." On the other hand, the *Ministry* of February, 1957, stated the very opposite. It said that the "sacrificial act on the cross (is) a complete, perfect and **final** atonement for men's sins." *Questions on Doctrine* attempts to reconcile these opposing views by stating that whether one "hears an Adventist say or reads in Adventist literature—even in the writings of Ellen G. White—that Christ is making atonement now, it should be understood that we mean simply that Christ is now making application," etc. pp. 354, 355. It is clear that if the atonement on the cross was **final**, there cannot be a later atonement also final. When we therefore for a hundred years have preached that the day of atonement began in 1844, we were wrong. It **ended** 1800 years before. The hundreds of books we have published; the more than a million copies of *Bible Readings* we have sold; the millions of hand bills we have distributed saying that it is "court week in Heaven," were false doctrine; the Bible instruction we have given the children and the young ministry and which they have imbibed as Bible truth, is a fable. Uriah Smith, Loughborough, Andrews, Andross, Watson, Daniells, Branson, Johnson, Lacey, Spicer, Haskell, Gilbert, and a host of others stand convicted of having taught false doctrine; and the whole denomination whose chief contribution to Christianity is the sanctuary doctrine and Christ's ministry, must now confess that we were all wrong, and that we have no message to the world for these last days. In other words, we are a deceived and deceiving people. The fact that we may have been honest does not alter the fact that we have given a false message. Take away from us the sanctuary question, the investigative judgment, the message of the 2300 days, Christ's work in the most holy, and we have no right to exist as a denominated people, as God's messengers to a doomed world. If the Spirit of Prophecy has led us astray these many years, let us throw it away.

But no! Halt! God has not led us astray. We have not told cunningly devised fables. We have a message that will stand the test and confound the undermining theories that are finding their way in among us. In this instance it is not the people that have gone astray except as they have followed the leaders. It is time that there be a turnabout.

It is now more than four years ago that the apostasy began to be plainly evident. Since that time there has been a deliberate attempt to weaken the faith in the Spirit of Prophecy, as it is clear that as long as the people revere the gift given us, they cannot be led far astray. Of this we shall speak shortly. The time for action has come. The time to open up the dark corners has arrived. There must no longer be any secret agreements, no compact with other denominations who hate the law and the Sabbath, who riducule our most holy faith. We must no longer hobnob with enemies of the truth, no more promise that we will not proselytize. We must not tolerate leadership which condones tampering with the writings entrusted to us, and stigmatizes as belonging to the lunatic fringe those who dare disagree with them. We must no longer remain silent. To thy tents, O Israel!

Be of good courage, brethren. The Lord still lives. We have a work to do. Let us all work together. And let us not forget that our greatest strength lies in close union with God, in prayer. Let us all dedicate ourselves anew to Him.

Letter No. 3

DOWNGRADING MRS. WHITE

Years ago while traveling in northern Minnesota, I stayed one weekend in a small town, as there was no train service on Sunday and buses did not exist. I did not like to remain idle so I arranged for the use of the Town Hall with the intent of holding a public service. I posted a handwritten notice that I would speak in the afternoon on the topic of "Seventh-day Adventists." I confess that I would rather not have spoken, for I needed a rest. My posted notice would certainly not draw many people.

To my surprise the hall was well-filled. As the people showed interest in the subject, I decided to appoint another service for the evening. Promptly a well-dressed man arose in the audience, introduced himself as the temporary pastor of the only church in town, and invited me to come over to his church and speak in the evening. I reminded him of my topic, but he stated that this was satisfactory and I could come over and speak on Adventism. I thanked him and accepted the invitation.

After the meeting that night he told me that he was almost sorry he had invited me. "When I heard you this after noon," he said, "I thought you were an intelligent man. Now I know you are not."

"What made you change your mind?"

"You said you believed in Genesis."

"Don't you?"

"Of course not. No intelligent man believes in the Genesis creation story."

"You don't believe in the Old Testament, then?"

"No intelligent man does."

"Do you believe in the New?"

"Well, yes, there are many good things in it. But when it comes to Paul, I draw the line. He is the cause of all our troubles."

"What about Christ?"

"Good man, very good man. Of course he had his faults. But he was a good man."

"Are you not a minister?"

"Yes, in a way. I am president of the (Blank) Seminary. I am up here on my vacation and am temporarily substituting for the pastor here in town, one of my former students."

This led to a conversation that lasted most of the night, and was very illuminating to me. I was somewhat acquainted with his institution, and one of my teachers was attending some classes there. "Do you teach your students what you have told me tonight?"

"Yes, and much more."

"And do your students tell their congregations?" Oh, my no! That would never do. The people are not ready for it. They are much more conservative than the preachers. We have to move slowly with them."

This episode came to mind as I have considered the situation in our denomination of late years. I have been uneasy since I first heard that our leaders were negotiating with the Evangelicals; but I had hoped that the blandishment of our church's being reckoned among the established churches as being one of them would not appeal to our men. We had heard too many sermons on the text, "The people shall dwell alone, and shall not be reckoned among the nations," to be deceived. (Numbers 23:9). As the negotiations were considered top secret it was some time before any definite news leaked out. When it did, it was disturbing. Washington furnished little news, and all others informed me they had nothing to say. It seemed apparent, however, our leaders were being influenced and steps were being taken that would be hard to retrace.

The first authentic news did not come from our leaders or through our journals but from an Evangelical publication dated September, 1956, which issued a special edition with an account of what had taken place. This account was so unbelievable that we hesitated to give it credence. We were sure that what it reported had never taken place and that our leaders would promptly issue a denial. We waited a year, we waited two. But until this date, no protest or denial has been issued. Reluctantly, we must, therefore, accept the account as true. Let us consider the situation as it has developed.

OUR LEADING JOURNALS

As I read the *Review and Herald* from week to week, I find the articles generally helpful. The contributors quote freely from the Spirit of Prophecy, as do the editors and feature writers. There are times when I disagree with certain positions which I consider unsound, but this is not often. There are at times reports that savor of boasting, and at other times much stress is laid on statistics. But I have learned not to take too seriously some minor matters. I read the *Review and Herald* with confidence; I enjoy it. I can say the same for the *Signs of the Times*.

But not so with the *Ministry*, our ministerial journal. The general articles are of the same kind and quality as the *Review and Herald*, but this is not always so with the special features and editorials. Them I must read carefully and critically. At times they contain what I consider heresy and dangerous perversions of truth. This may seem a serious charge. And it is so intended. I can best illustrate what I have in mind by presenting a concrete example.

THE *MINISTRY*

Of late years there has been a definite change of emphasis in the *Ministry*, and not for the better. This change coincides with the period in which our leaders have been in close contact and rapport with the Evangelicals. The trend was in evidence before, but now has blossomed. As an example of this, I shall call attention to an article in the February, 1957, issue entitled, **"The Priestly Application of the Atoning Act."** It is claimed that it "is the Adventist understanding of the atonement, confirmed and illustrated and clarified by the Spirit of Prophecy." As it has not been renounced or protested, we may justly conclude that it is officially approved.

THE ATONEMENT

The author gives a short tribute to the "magnifying glass," the Spirit of Prophecy, then goes on to state that the atonement "…is not, on the one hand, limited just to the sacrificial death of Christ on the cross. On the other hand, neither is it confined to the ministry of our heavenly High Priest in the sanctuary above, on the antitypical day of atonement—or hour of God's judgment—as some of our forefathers first erroneously thought and wrote." *Ministry*, February, 1957, p. 9. The author stresses the fact that the Spirit of Prophecy clearly teaches that both these aspects are included, "…one aspect being incomplete without the other, and each being the indispensable complement of the other." *Ibid.* That is, both the death on the cross and Christ's ministry in the second apartment are necessary to the atonement. With this, we are in full agreement. The death was a necessary part of the atonement. The one is incomplete without the other.

This point should be noted, for a few sentences further on the author will say that the death on the cross is **complete in itself**; to quote: "The sacrificial act of the cross (is) a **complete, perfect and final** atonement for man's sin." Page 10. After having first said that the sacrificial death was incomplete, he now says it is **complete,**

perfect, and final. He does not consider the death merely as a **partial** atonement, but a **complete** and perfect and final one. With this we disagree. The two statements are irreconcilable.

This is more than merely an unfortunate wording. While in the next paragraph the author gives lip service to the need of a ministration in the sanctuary above, he leaves out every essential feature of the atonement and omits the dates which are essential to the Adventist concept of the atonement, which justifies our existence as a denominated people with the message for the world at this time.

In his explanation of Christ's work in the sanctuary, he does not refer to or mention Daniel 8:14: "Then shall the sanctuary be cleansed." Without this text, Christ's work in the sanctuary becomes meaningless. He does not mention 457 B.C. or the 70 weeks, or the middle of the week which pinpoints the time of the sacrifice on the cross, and is "...as a nail in a sure place," (Isaiah 22:23) to which we fasten the whole chronological scheme in prophecy and which also justifies the date, 1844. Remove or change these dates, and Adventists are without an anchor for the chronological system climaxing in 1844, and are unable to justify their existence as a people who are to proclaim this most important message to the world for this time: "Fear God, and give glory to him; for the hour of his judgment is come." (Revelation 14:7). Every one of these dates the author leaves out, and what remains, in the words of Dr. Barnhouse, "is **flat, stale** and **unprofitable**." *Eternity* Extra, September, 1956, p. 4.

A COMPREHENSIVE ASSEMBLAGE

In *Questions on Doctrine*, beginning at page 661, there is a section C consisting of collections from the writings of Sister White on the subject of **atonement**, thirty pages in all. It claims to be a "comprehensive assemblage" of Sister White's teachings on the atonement. From the use of the word, "comprehensive," I expected to find a full and extensive collection. But in consulting this material, I was disappointed in its paucity and one-sidedness. I found it to be a very incomplete and meager collection, leaving out numerous quotations that rightly belong even in a small compilation, not to say a comprehensive one. And strangely enough, quotations that were omitted were such as must on no account be left out.

First of all, I wanted to know what Sister White had to say of the date, 1844, which is the "crisis year." I wanted to know if it had anything particularly to do with the atonement, or if it could safely be left out. I found that the author had omitted it. So I looked in turn for other quotations, not one of which I found in the assemblage. I looked for the statement: "At the termination of the 2300 days in 1844...our great High Priest...enters the holy of holies, and there appears in the presence of God, to...perform the work of the **investigative judgment**, and to make **an atonement** for all who are shown to be entitled to its benefits." This is said to be the "great day of **final** atonement." *Great Controversy*, p. 480. I searched for this important statement in the comprehensive assemblage, but it was not there. I looked for the parallel statement: "...at the termination of the 2300 days in 1844, Christ entered the most holy place of the heavenly sanctuary to perform the **closing work of atonement**, preparatory to His coming. *Ibid.,* p. 442. I did not find it. I looked for this statement: "...this is the service which began when the 2300 days ended. At that time, as foretold by Daniel the prophet, our High Priest entered the most holy, to perform the **last division** of His solemn work—to cleanse the sanctuary." I could not find it. I looked for the statement: "The end of the 2300 days in 1844 marked an **important crisis**." *Ibid.* p 429. I did not find it. I looked for other statements, such as: "The sacred work of Christ (that) is **going on at the present time in the heavenly sanctuary**," "...the atoning work of Christ is **now in progress** in the heavenly sanctuary," "**Today** He is making atonement for us before the Father." *Testimonies*, Vol. p. 520; *White Board Minutes*, p. 1483; *MS. 21*, 1895, quoted in *Ministry*, February, 1957, p. 30. I found none of these.

At first I thought that this book, *Questions on Doctrine*, did not have room for these texts, nor did the *Ministry*. But I had to abandon this reasoning when I observed that it was only a particular kind of statements that was omitted. The omitted quotations all clustered about the important **"crisis"** date, 1844, the **investigative judgment**, Christ's entering into the most holy for the **final atonement**: His making atonement **now**: His making atonement **"today before the Father."** These are the statements that Dr. Barnhouse ridiculed and which he said our leaders had "totally repudiated." He had also ridiculed Hiram Edson's experience in the cornfield and had called the investigative judgment not only a "peculiar" but a "human, face-saving idea," in fact "the most co-lossal, psychological, face-saving phenomenon in religious history." *Eternity* Extra, September, 1956, pp. 3, 4. And now we found all these offending statements left out of the "comprehensive assemblage." Can this be a mere coincidence?

We wonder what effect the ridicule of the Evangelicals had upon our leaders and upon the author of the article in the *Ministry*, which we are discussing. One thing that kept our men from going overboard, body and soul, to the Evangelicals, was, doubtless, Mrs. White's writings. She is very emphatic on the question of the sanctuary, and it would not be easy to convert our people to the new view, as long as they had the *Testimonies* to sustain them in the old position. The faith of our people in the Spirit of Prophecy must be weakened, or better yet, destroyed, before much headway can be made in bringing in the new view. The *Ministry* article serves well for this purpose.

It was **the editor**, himself, who in his research had "become acutely aware of the E. G. White statements which indicate that the atoning work of Christ is now in progress in the heavenly sanctuary." *White Minutes*, p. 1483. This did not at all fit in with the new view that the atonement was made on the cross, and so he suggested that "footnotes or Appendix notes might appear in certain of the E. G. White books clarifying very largely in the words of Ellen White our understanding of the various phases of the atoning work of Christ." *Ibid.* And he suggested haste in the "preparation and inclusion of such notes in future printings of the E. G. White books." When the plan became known, it was abandoned. The author of the article in the February, 1957, *Ministry* then took over and had the article printed which we are considering.

NOT IN A SINGLE CASE

The author asks this question, "Why, in the early days, in the light of all this, did not Mrs. White point out and correct the limited or sometimes erroneous concept of some of our early writers concerning the atonement? And why did she employ some of their restricted phrases without contrasting, at the time, her own larger, truer meaning when using them?" *Ministry*, February, 1957, P. 11.

This was the dilemma: Some of our early writers had erroneous concepts about the atonement, the author claims. Sister White did not correct them, but even used some of their own restricted phrases. How could this be explained? The answer, which the author gives, is the most astonishing and astounding answer that has ever been given to such a question. Hear this:

"In answer: it is essential that we first of all remember this basic fact: **No doctrinal truth or prophetic Interpretation ever came to this people initially through the Spirit of Prophecy—not in a single case.**" (Emphasis his.)

Read those words again. And have in mind that this is an article which claims to give the true meaning of the atonement, the official interpretation; that it has the approval of the administration and that the editor passed it. Also, it has not been retracted or changed. It stands.

These are bold words, almost unbelievable words, and utterly untrue words. To assert that Sister White never, not even in a single case, initially contributed any doctrinal truth or prophetic interpretation will not be believed by her thousands and millions of readers who all have been benefited by her works. For myself, I have been greatly helped and instructed by her doctrinal teachings and prophetic interpretation. Even the author himself, who on page 11 of the February, 1957, *Ministry*, says, "We are fundamentally Protestants, taking the Bible only as our sole rule of faith and practice," in a signed letter the next month asserts, "I take the total Spirit of Prophecy teachings on a given subject to be the authoritative Seventh-day Adventist teaching." It does not strengthen faith to have a writer say publicly, "The Bible and the Bible only" and privately deny it. One statement is evidently made to the world for them to believe; the other to our people to quiet their fears. Some explanation is due.

The reader will have noted that the author does not say that Sister White never contributed any doctrinal truth or prophetic interpretation. He says that she never contributed anything **initially**, that is, she never made any original contribution. She got it from somebody else, she "lifted" it. Our enemies have made that assertion for years, but I never thought that such would be announced to the whole world with the consent of the leaders. But here it is. Whatever Sister White wrote, be it the counsel of Father and Son in eternity, or Satan's inmost rebellious thoughts, "somebody told her." **She** never contributed a thing, initially. Never in a single case! Let me produce a **single** case. The following is taken from *Testimonies for the Church, Series B, No. 2,* pp. 56, 57.

"Many of our people do not realize how firmly the foundation of our faith has been laid. My husband, Elder Joseph Bates, Father Pierce, Elder Edson, and others who were keen, noble, and true, were among those who after the passing of the time in 1844, searched for the truth as for hidden treasure. I met with them, and we studied and prayed earnestly. Often we remained together until late at night, and sometimes through the entire night, praying for light and studying the word. Again and again these brethren came together to study the Bible, in order that we might know its meaning, and be prepared to teach it with power. When they came to the point in their study where they said, 'We can do nothing more,' the Spirit of the Lord would come upon me. I would be taken off in vision, and a clear explanation of the passages we had been studying would be given me, with instruction as to how we were to labor and teach effectively. **Thus light was given** that helped us to understand the Scriptures in regard to **Christ, His mission,** and **His priesthood.** A line of truth extending from that time to the time when we shall enter the city of God, was made plain to me, and **I gave others the instruction that the Lord had given me.**"

In this case there was no human intermediary. Unless we are to believe that Sister White did not tell the truth, she got her instructions from above. In this case the instruction concerned **"Christ, His mission, and His priesthood,"** the very subjects we have now under consideration. Whatever we may be, or not be, sure of, we know now that the instruction that came to Sister White on the subject of Christ, His mission and His priesthood came direct from God. This means that the sanctuary question as our forefathers taught and believed it has God for its author. It came as a result of a vision, which I do not believe can be said of any other doctrine we hold.

A CRISIS

We have reached a crisis in this denomination when leaders are attempting to enforce false doctrine and threaten those who object. The whole program is unbelievable. Men are now attempting to remove the foundations of many generations, and think they can succeed. If we did not have the Spirit of Prophecy we would not know of the departure from sound doctrine which is now threatening us, and the coming of the Omega which will decimate our ranks and cause grievous wounds. The present situation has been clearly outlined. We are nearing the climax.

I am well aware that oftentimes visions were given to confirm previous study. I am well aware that for some time Sister White's mind was "locked," as she expressed it, and that hence visions were given, as in the instance here considered. She herself says that "for two or three years my mind continued to be locked to an understanding of the Scriptures." During that time the Lord gave visions. Then an experience came to her, and she records, "...from that time to this I have been able to understand the word of God." *Ibid.* p. 58. For "two or three years" Mrs. White's mind was locked. This was evidently intended by God to strengthen their faith in the gift; for the men knew that of herself she had no knowledge. Then, when they came to the end of their knowledge and did not know what to do, light came from a Source of which they knew that of herself she could not solve their problems. It was clearly the Lord's leading, and they confessed it and "accepted as light from Heaven the revelations given."

In an attempt to protect himself, the author now turns completely around and says that she frequently went "far beyond the positions taken by any of the original advocates, and her counsels would often be so clear, so full, and so far reaching that they proved to be far ahead of the concepts of any of her contemporaries—sometimes fifty years in advance of their acceptance by some." I wonder whom she copied under such circumstances?

In composing the book, *Questions on Doctrine*, it became necessary to do some research work in Sister White's published and unpublished manuscripts to ascertain beyond a doubt just what she had said on various matters. This work was turned over to the *Ministry* author who reports as follows in the *Ministry* for February, 1957, p. 11:

The *Ministry* Report

"The further question has likewise arisen: 'Just why were these counsels, clarifications, and expositions on the atonement, and its priestly manifestations, not brought together for our use before this?' The answer, we believe, is equally simple and straightforward and obvious: **No one had taken the time for the sustained effort involved in laborious, comprehensive search necessary to find, analyze, and organize them.**

"Since our leaders were largely unaware of this latent evidence and its priceless value, the **need was not felt**, and the time required for such a vast project was not considered available. Access to the complete files of all the old periodicals containing Ellen White's two thousand articles is not easy, for there is no complete file in any one place. More than that, the priceless manuscript statements are not available in published form.[2]

"Further, as a church we have been so engrossed in giving our special message to the world, in keeping with our complex movement rolling onward in its multiple activities, **that no one seemed to have the time or even the burden for such a huge task. It was known that the search would be a most laborious one because of the vast amount of material that must be compassed.**

"However, when the need clearly arose and the time for such a search had obviously come, the necessity was recognized and the time taken to compass not only the familiar book statements, but the vast array of periodicals, articles, and manuscript counsels bearing thereon."

It will be noted that the author does not minimize the task that faced him—and it **was** a great task. It is to be regretted that he should take the opportunity to inform us that the leaders had not felt the need of this work, did not have the time for it, and did not even have any burden for it.

It was in this research that he discovered that Mrs. White did not contradict or change what she said in the beginning of her work. The author puts it in his peculiar phraseology that, "Mrs. White's later statements do not contradict or change her earlier expressions." He had evidently hoped that she had changed her position on the atonement, which position he had criticized and attempted to explain by saying that she never, not even in a single case, had contributed anything initially to doctrine or prophetic interpretation. It is clear that if she intended to change her position, she had abundant opportunity to do so in the sixty or more years she lived after making her position clear on the atonement. But she did not contradict or change what she

---

2   However, now most are available in printed form as well as on CD-ROM.

had once written. This is the testimony of the very one who had challenged her early position, and who now is compelled to testify that she did not change. It is a poetic justice that the author of the *Ministry* article should be the one to testify after he had examined all the material there is no evidence that she ever changed her mind or contradicted what she had written earlier.

This created another dilemma for our author. He must now let stand all she had ever written, and could not argue that she had authorized any change whatsoever. What then could he do or did he do? A most unique solution he had: he calmly asserted that **Sister White did not mean what she said**! Note again his peculiar use of the English language, not a direct statement but a passive approach: he says, "…a distinct clarification of terms and of **meaning emerges** that is destined to have far-reaching consequences." Her later statements "invest those earlier terms with a larger, truer **meaning** inherently there all the time." And so he explains when she says that Christ is making atonement (he is omitting the word **now**, she is "obviously **meaning applying** the completed atonement to the individual." [Emphasis his.]

This is in complete harmony with the statement in *Questions on Doctrine* where the author boldly asserts that if any one "hears an Adventist say, or reads in Adventist literature—even in the writings of Ellen White—that Christ is making atonement now, it should be understood that we **mean** simply that Christ is **making application of the benefits of the sacrificial atonement He made on the cross**."

This is news indeed. I have written several books, one of them on the Sanctuary service and hence these may come under what he calls "Adventist literature." And now some unauthorized individual proclaims to the world that when I say that Christ is making atonement now, I do not mean it. I mean that He is making **application**, but not atonement which was made 1800 years ago. However, it is only a minor matter that he presumes to act as my interpreter and tell what I mean by what I say. But when he undertakes to tell the world that when Sister White says Christ is making atonement she means simply that He is making **application**, that is serious. God's reproof to Job when he was talking too much may apply here: "Who is this that darkeneth counsel by words without knowledge?" (Job 38:1). It is not often that God is sarcastic. But here He is. Read verse 21. Job deserved it.

And so when I read, "... even in the writings of Ellen G. White," that Christ is making atonement, I am not to believe it. He made the atonement 1800 years ago, not now; and even if she affirms that Christ is making atonement **now**, that "**today** He is making atonement," that "We are in the great day of atonement, and the sacred work of Christ for the people of God that is going on at the present time (1882) in the heavenly sanctuary should be our constant study," I am still to apply to the interpreter to find out what she means. *Testimonies to the Church, Vol. 5*, p. 250.

Such is playing with words, it is playing with fire, and makes any interpretation possible. If the author is right, I am permitted to take any word of an author and say that he means something else than what he says. Such makes intercommunication impossible, and the world a Babel. What would agreements amount to, or contracts, or words of mouth, if I am permitted to put my own interpretation on what another man says? The Bible says that the seventh day is the Sabbath. That seems plain enough. But the author's theory would permit me to hold that the Bible means no such thing. Absurd, you say. And I say Amen. When the Bible says **seven**, it does not mean **one**. With the author's philosophy, however, words become meaningless. "Let your nay be nay, and your yea, yea," James says. That is, mean what you say. To make the plain statement that "Christ is making **atonement** now" means that He is making **application** now is indefensible on grammatical, philological, theological, or common-sense ground. And to go farther and upon such false interpretation build a new theology to be enforced by sanctions, is simply out of this world. Undue assumption of authority coupled with overconfidence in the virtue of bestowed honors have born fruit. And the fruit is not good.

The present attempt to lessen and destroy confidence in the Spirit of Prophecy and establish a new theology, may deceive some, even many, but the foundations upon which we have built these many years, still stand, and God still lives. This warning should not go unheeded: "If you lessen the confidence of God's people in the testimonies He has sent them, you are rebelling against God as certainly as were Korah, Dathan, and Abiram." *Testimonies to the Church*, Vol. 5, p. 66.

In an incomplete research which I conducted years ago I found what the author found, and more. Among other things, I found in a small pamphlet entitled, *"A Word to the Little Flock,"* published by

James White in Brunswick, Maine, May 30, 1847, a statement by Sister White on the sanctuary that immediately drew my attention. It is dated April 21, 1847, and written from Topsham, Maine. On page 12, I found these words, which I suppose our *Ministry* author also found. Says Sisterr.White:

> "I believe the sanctuary, to be cleansed at the end of the 2300 days, is the New Jerusalem Temple, of which Christ is a minister. The Lord shew (showed) me in vision, more than a year ago, that **Brother Crosier had the true light** on the cleansing of the sanctuary, etc., and that it was His will, that Brother C (Crosier) should write out the view which he gave us in the *Day-Star Extra,* February 7, 1846. **I feel fully authorized by the Lord, to recommend that Extra to every saint.** I pray that these lines may prove a blessing to you, and to all the dear children who may read them. Signed, E. G. White."

I lost no time to get a copy of that *Extra* and read it. As I write this I have before me a photostatic copy of the *Day-Star Extra* for February 7, 1846, and on pages 40 and 41 of that issue I read Brother Crosier's article. After having discussed certain theories in which he does not believe, Brother Crosier observes:

CROSIER SPEAKS

"But again, they say the atonement was made and finished on Calvary when the Lamb of God expired. So men have taught us, and so the churches and the world believe; but it is none the more true or sacred on that account, if unsupported by Divine authority. Perhaps few or none who hold that opinion have ever tested the foundation on which it rests.

"1. If the atonement was made on Calvary, by whom was it made? The making of the atonement is the work of a priest; but who officiated on Calvary? Roman soldiers and wicked Jews.

"2. The **slaying** was not making the atonement; the sinner slew the victim. Lev. 4:1–4, 13–15, etc., after that the priest took the blood and made the atonement. Lev. 4:5–12, 16–21.

"3. Christ was the appointed High Priest to make the atonement, and certainly could not have acted in that capacity till after His resurrection, and we have no record of His doing anything on earth after His resurrection which could be called the atonement.

"4. The atonement was made in the sanctuary, but Calvary was not such a place.

"5. He could not, according to Heb. 8:4 make the atonement while on earth. 'If He were on earth, He could not be a priest.' The Levitical was the earthly priesthood; the Divine, the heavenly.

"6. Therefore, He did not begin the work of making the atonement, whatever the nature of that work may be, till after His ascension, when by His own blood He entered the heavenly sanctuary for us."

This, then is the "true light," which the Lord showed Sister White in vision, had His approval, and which she felt fully authorized to recommend to every saint. Only as we downgrade Sister White can we reject this testimony of hers. We are not ready to do this.

We now face this situation: Did our *Ministry* author in his thorough search find this statement that Brother Crosier had "the true light?" If he did not find it, he has little ground to feel pleased with his work. In either case, if I were a teacher and had sent him to do this research work and he presented the collection in *Questions on Doctrine* as his report, I would have to give him a straight F, which in school language stands for Failure. It is either a case of poor research, or of omission, which latter, under the circumstances, is most serious.

Letter No. 4
A RÉSUMÉ

In the documents and letters I have sent out from time to time concerning what I consider a serious departure from the faith on the part of the leaders, I have adhered strictly to the advice which Christ gives in Matthew 18:15–17. There He says that if differences arise among brethren, "tell him his fault between thee and him alone." If he will not hear, "take with thee one or two more, that in the mouth of two or three witnesses every word may be established. And if he shall neglect to hear them, tell it unto the church." This principle I have followed as will appear from the record.

In the month of May, 1957, there was placed in my hand, providentially I believe, a copy of the *Minutes* of the White Board of Trustees for May 1 and 2, 1957, recording a meeting of two brethren with the Trustees concerning a statement they had found in Mrs. White's writings regarding the atonement. They sought counsel in this matter, inasmuch as what they had found did not harmonize with the new view which the leaders were advocating. What attitude should these researchers take in view of Mrs. White's statement?

For a number of months, even for years, our leaders had been studying with some evangelical ministers with a view to eventual recognition of the Adventists as an evangelical Christian body. The studies were concerning the doctrines of the Adventists, particularly the Atonement, the Investigative judgment, and Christ's work in the heavenly sanctuary since 1844. These doctrines the evangelicals had called "the most colossal, psychological, face-saving phenomenon in religious history," and had so denominated them in their journal, *Eternity*, for September, 1956, reprinting the article in an *Extra* under the title, "Are Seventh-day Adventists Christians?"

The evangelical ministers appear to have made a pronounced impression upon the Adventist leaders, so much so that Dr. Barnhouse, one of the participating evangelical ministers, reports that the Adventist leaders "totally repudiated" some of their most important doctrines. It may be best to let Dr. Barnhouse tell the story himself as he reported it in the *Extra* named above, for September, 1956. The particular subject which he discusses is what is called "The Great Disappointment," and has reference to the great disappointment of the

43

Adventists in 1844 when they expected the Lord to come. Here is his account:

"On the morning after the 'Great Disappointment' two men were going through a corn field in order to avoid the pitiless gaze of their mocking neighbors to whom they had said an eternal goodbye the day before. To put it in the words of Hiram Edson (the man in the corn field who first conceived this peculiar idea), he was overwhelmed with the conviction 'that instead of our High Priest **coming out** of the Most Holy of the heavenly sanctuary to come to this earth on the tenth day of the seventh month at the end of the 2,300 days, He for the first time **entered** on that day the **second** apartment of that sanctuary, and that He had work to perform in the Most Holy before coming to this earth.' It is to my mind, therefore, nothing more than a human, face-saving idea. It should also be realized that some uninformed Seventh-day Adventists took this idea and carried it to fantastic, literalistic extremes. Mr. Martin and I heard the Adventist leaders say, flatly, that they repudiate all such extremes. This they have said in no uncertain terms. Further, they do not believe, as some of their earlier teachers taught, that Jesus' atoning work was not completed on Calvary, but instead that He was still carrying on a second ministering work since 1844. This idea is also totally repudiated. They believe that since His ascension Christ has bean ministering the benefits of the atonement which He completed on Calvary.

"Since the sanctuary doctrine is based on the type of the Jewish high priest going into the Holy of Holies to complete his atoning work, it can be seen that what remains is most certainly exegetically untenable and theological speculation of a highly imaginative order. What Christ is now doing, since 1844, according to this version, is going over the records of all human beings and deciding what rewards are going to be given to individual Christians. We personally do not believe that there is even a suspicion of a verse in Scripture to sustain such a peculiar position, and we further believe that any effort to establish it is **stale, flat,** and **unprofitable**!" (Emphasis in original.)

In explanation of this somewhat involved statement, I append the following explanation, which may clarify some expressions.

Dr. Barnhouse first reports the well-known incident of Hiram Edson going through the cornfield on the morning after the "Disappointment," and becoming convinced that "instead of our High Priest **coming out** of the Most Holy ... He for the first time **entered** on that day the second apartment of that sanctuary, and that He had a work to perform in the Most Holy before coming to this earth." The work He was to do before coming to this earth was the completion of the atonement which involved the investigative judgment. This conception, says Dr. Barnhouse, "is nothing more than a human, face-saving idea." Then he continues, "Some uninformed Seventh-day Adventists took this idea and carried it to fantastic, literalistic extremes." That is, they believed that Christ really did go into the Most Holy to do a work which had to be done before His coming to this earth, which involved the investigative judgment and the completion of the atonement. Dr. Barnhouse reports: "Mr. Martin and I heard the Adventist leaders say, flatly, that they repudiate all such extremes. This they have said in no uncertain terms."

If we are to believe Dr. Barnhouse's statement, then our leaders repudiated a doctrine which we have held sacred from the beginning. This is made clear as Dr. Barnhouse continues: "Some of their earlier teachers taught that Jesus' atoning work was not completed on Calvary, but instead that He was still carrying on a second ministerial work since 1844. This idea is also totally repudiated."

When Dr. Barnhouse says that "some" of our earlier teachers taught "that Jesus' atoning work was not completed on Calvary," he must have gotten his information from some of the "uninformed" authors of our new theology; for history records that all our teachers taught this. James White, J. H. Waggoner, Uriah Smith, J. N. Andrews, J. N. Loughborough, C. H. Watson, E. E. Andross, W. H. Branson, Camden Lacey, R. S. Owen, O. A. Johnson, H. R. Johnson, F. D. Nichols, (until 1955) all stoutly defended the doctrine of Christ's atoning work since 1844, and committed their convictions to writing. As I write this, I have nearly all their books before me. James White, our first General Conference president, when he was elected the first editor of *Signs of the Times*, wrote in the first issue of that paper an article "to correct false statements circulated against us... There are many who call themselves Adventists, who hold views with which we can have no sympathy, some of which, we think, are subversive of the plainest and most important principles set forth in the word of God." The second of the twenty-five articles of faith reads in part as follows: Christ "lived our example, died our sacrifice, was raised for our justification, ascended on high, to be our only mediator in the sanctuary in Heaven, where, with his own blood, he makes atonement for our sins; which atonement, **so far from being made on the cross**, which was but the offering of the sacrifice, is the very last portion of his work as priest." These **Fundamental Beliefs**, were also printed in a little tract and circulated by the thousands. It would be interesting if the one who wrote pages 29, 30, 31, 32, in *Questions on Doctrine*, would furnish us with a list of writers who held views contrary to those of the authors mentioned above. I have not found any proof for the incorrect statements found on those particular pages.

To continue our study of Dr. Barnhouse's report in the *Eternity Extra:* He has just affirmed that the Adventist leaders have "totally repudiated" the idea that Christ is "still carrying on a second ministering work since 1844," by which he means an atoning work. Instead of this, he says, "they believe that since His ascension Christ has been ministering the benefits of the atonement which He completed on Calvary." This view, however, he does not consider consistent. The Old Testament informs us that the high priest killed the sacrifice in the court outside the tabernacle. But the **killing was not the atonement**. "It is the *blood* that maketh atonement." (Leviticus 17:11). Therefore the high priest shall "bring his **blood** within the veil...and sprinkle it upon the mercy seat and before the mercy seat, and he shall make an atonement for the holy place." (Leviticus 16:15, 16). "He **goeth in** to make an atonement." (Verse 17). Dr. Barnhouse argues, that as we base our doctrine of atonement largely on the figure given us in Leviticus, and use that in our teaching on the atonement, we must believe that as the high priest on earth took the blood into the sanctuary and there made atonement, so Christ must do likewise, He must **go in** to complete the atonement. Else we have an atonement without blood. If we do not take the last step, then we are compelled to believe that the atonement was made in the court and not in the sanctuary, which completely destroys all typology. If this last service with the blood is omitted, then our theory of the atonement is sadly incomplete, and "is most certainly exegetically untenable, and theological speculation of a highly imaginative order." **If Christ does not go in with the blood to**

complete the atonement, then what we have left "is **stale, flat,** and **unprofitable**." He has a good argument.

IS IT TRUE?

When I first read in the *Extra* that our leaders had repudiated the doctrine of Christ's atoning work in the sanctuary since 1844, and had substituted for this "the application of the benefits of the sacrificial atonement He made on the cross," I could not believe it, and did not believe it. When I was told that even if I read in "the writings of Ellen G. White, that Christ is making atonement **now**," I am not to believe it, I wondered, "What are we coming to?" The atonement was made 1800 years ago, our leaders say. Sr. White says the atonement is going on **now**. *Questions on Doctrine* says it was made 1800 years ago. The *Ministry* says the atonement on the cross was final. Whom or what am I to believe? To me, to repudiate Christ's ministry in the second apartment, **now**, is to repudiate Adventism. That is one of the foundation pillars of Adventism. If we reject the atonement in the sanctuary now, we may as well repudiate all Adventism. For this, God's people are not ready. They will not follow the leaders in apostasy.

At this juncture it occurred to me that perhaps the *Eternity* men had regretted what they had written and had retracted, or would retract, all they had written. So I wrote to *Eternity*, asking if they still published the *Extra*. They answered that they did. The article being copyrighted, I than asked for permission to quote them. I received this answer: "We are glad to give you permission to quote from the article, 'Are Seventh-day Adventists Christians?' and would appreciate you giving credit to *Eternity* when you do this." This letter was dated Philadelphia, Pennsylvania, May 2, 1958, and signed by the editor.

This was twenty months after the article had first appeared in *Eternity*. If at any time during those twenty months our leaders had protested, if they had made a demurrer, in honesty the editor would have warned me not to use the material, and not to quote these statements. But the editor did no such thing. He was glad and willing for me to use the material, willing to stand by what the *Extra* had published, willing for me to quote them. It is fully five years since the discussions began, and three years since the *Extra* was published. For this long time I have been waiting for our men to deny the charges, and rebuke the evangelicals for publishing such defamation of our entire leadership. But I have heard no protest. On the contrary, I have read several references in our papers to these evangelicals as being fine, Christian gentlemen, which I believe is true. Such men do not tell falsehoods. In the absence of any denial or protest from our men, I have reluctantly drawn my own conclusions. But if our men will make a straightforward declaration that Dr. Barnhouse and Mr. Martin never heard them make such statements as *Eternity* avers, I will immediately get in contact with the evangelicals and ask them to make apologies for such serious and grave accusations. This matter is too serious to go by default. Thousands of our people have read the *Eternity* article and are seriously concerned . One of the main pillars of our faith has, according to *Eternity*, been removed. Shall we stand idly by and permit the sanctuary to be trodden under foot, and that by its supposed supporters?

THE VAULT INCIDENT

We shall now return to the two men who entered the White vault in May, 1957, to counsel with the White Trustees. They had finished their research work, and reported to the board that they had found "indications" that Sr. White taught that "the atoning work of Christ is now (1880) in progress in the heavenly sanctuary." This discovery was a deathblow to their new theology. It was evidently impossible to believe that the work of atonement was completed on the cross and was final, and also to teach that it was still in progress in Heaven. Both statements could not be true. However, the denomination had already committed itself on this point,—and had in 1957 published in the *Ministry* that the great act on the cross was "a complete, perfect, and final atonement for man's sin." *Ministry*, February, 1957. The article said that this is now "the Adventist understanding of the atonement, confirmed, and illuminated and clarified by the Spirit of Prophecy." *Ibid.* This statement has never been retracted, or modified, or changed, and neither the writer nor the editor has been reproved. It stands.

In view of the situation, what were the researchers to do? They were faced with the statement of Mrs. White's, that the atonement is now in progress in Heaven. They were face to face with the other statement of the leaders that the atonement was made and finished on the cross. They must accept one or the other. They chose to go with the leaders.

But what about Sister White's statements, for there are many of them? It was clear that in some way her influence must be weakened and her statements watered down. But that was a delicate piece of work; and whatever was to be done had to be done in secret. If it were found out in time, the plan would not succeed. If, however, they could work in secret, and work rapidly, that matter would be a *"fait accompli"*—done before any one found out about it.

It was at this time that a copy of the White minutes were handed me. I shall now present the minutes, so that all may see for themselves what was done.

The *Minutes*, as of May 1, 1957, page 1483.

"At this juncture in our work, Elders X and Y were invited to join the Trustees in discussing further a matter that had been given study in January. Elder X and his group who have been studying with certain ministers have become acutely aware of E. G. White statements which indicate that the atoning work of Christ is now in progress in the heavenly sanctuary. In one statement in *Fundamentals of Christian Education*, the word "sacrifice" is used. To non-Adventists, unfamiliar with our understanding of the sanctuary question, references to a continuation of the atoning work of Christ, are difficult to grasp, and it was suggested to the Trustees that some footnotes or Appendix notes might appear in certain of the E. G. White books clarifying very largely in the words of Ellen White our understanding of the various phases of the atoning work of Christ. It was felt by the brethren who joined the Trustees in the discussion that this is a matter which will come prominently to the front in the near future, and that we would do well to move forward with the preparation and inclusion of such notes in future printings of the E. G. White's writings. The matter was discussed carefully and earnestly, but at the time that the meeting broke up to accommodate other committees, no action was taken."

Meeting, May 2. page 1488.
E. G. White Statements on the Atoning Work of Christ

"The meeting of the Trustees held May 1 closed with no action taken on the question which was discussed at length—suitable footnotes or explanations regarding the E. G. White statements on the atoning work of Christ which indicate a continuing work at the present time in Heaven. Inasmuch as the Chairman of our board will be away from Washington for the next four months, and the involvements in this question are such that it must have the most careful consideration and counsel,

"It was

VOTED, That we defer consideration until a later time of the matters that were brought to our attention by Elders X and Y involving the E. G. White statements concerning the continuing atoning work of Christ."

After the chairman of the board had returned from his four months' trip, the matter was further discussed, and it was decided not to grant the request. This action is worthy of commendation, but the praise is somewhat dimmed by the fact that it took eight months to come to this decision, and that they did not arrive at this conclusion until the plan had become known.

This report stunned me. How did anyone dare to suggest inclusions in Sister White's writings to bolster the new view? I pondered long, and prayed much. Did I have any responsibility in this matter? If I did, it would be my duty to speak to one man, and one only. As the transgression was not against me but against the church and our most holy faith, it was my duty to speak to our highest officer. This I did.

In my letter of February 27, 1957, I had voiced my fear of publishing the proposed book, *Questions on Doctrine*, it had been prepared altogether too hurriedly and after only a short time of study. Books of this kind cannot be written on short notice and should be prepared by men who have given a lifetime of study to the subject and spent years in research of the *Testimonies*.

March 7, 1957, I received this answer: "I notice your observation: 'I fear greatly for the contents of the book that is being published setting forth our belief.' I do not believe, Brother Andreasen, that you need to fear for what will appear in the book. It is being carefully gone over by a group of capable man in whom we have the utmost confidence. I feel quite confident you will be happy with the results."

In my answer of March 11, I again expressed my fear of the contents of the book. Referring to an article that appeared in the *Ministry*, February, 1957, I said: "If the committee agrees with his published views, I must most earnestly protest. For the views are most certainly not Adventist doctrine, but views derived from a superficial study of certain portions of the writings of Sr. White, and do not represent the general teachings." I finished with these words:

"I hereby lodge my protest against the publication at this time of any doctrine of the atonement, and wish my protest to be duly recorded. I can but feel that some of the brethren have been led into the present predicament by a desire to be like the nations around us (churches) and that we will yet rue the day when we began making concessions because of pressure from outside sources."

Receiving no answer, I wrote again May 10, 1957:

"I trust that you get the idea that I am in earnest. I have the utmost confidence in you. In my more than sixty years of official connection with the denomination, one of my chief aims has been to inspire confidence in the Spirit of Prophecy. The last two years I have spoken on the subject 204 times. I have felt that our people needed help, and I have tried to help them. I am heartbroken of what the future seems to hold unless God helps us. May the Lord give you both wisdom and courage to do what the situation demands."

After I had come into possession of the confidential minutes of the White Estate board, I followed Christ's instruction to "speak to him alone," and sent four letters to our chief officer. January 26, 1957, I received this answer:

"I am certain we can trust the brethren of the White Estate to move cautiously in this direction and not to take positions that might be embarrassing in the future. Certainly, Brother Andreasen, there is no intention here whatever to tamper with the writings of Sister White. We value them most highly.

"Referring to the book on *Questions and Answers* [same as *Questions on Doctrine*], let me assure you here, too, that this is not the work of the brethren whose names you mention. It is true that they did certain original work, but it was taken out of their hands and is the product of a large group of men rather than a few."

July 4, 1957, I answered. Here is part of this answer.

"I fear the day may come when this matter will become known to the people. It will shake the faith of the whole denomination. Of course, some will rejoice that at last Sr. White has been disposed of. Others will weep and cry to the Lord for consolation, 'Spare thy people, and give not thine heritage to reproach.' And when we are caught in our own net, will the churches of the world gloat? Please, brother, see to it that the proposed book is not published. It will be fatal. If there is no atoning work now going on in the sanctuary above, then the denomination may as well admit their mistake openly and fairly, and abide by the consequences. Let us throw Sr. White aside, and no longer hypocritically defend her writings, but behind the scenes edit them and still claim that they are her work. I close with an expression of high regard for you. You have an almost overwhelming task before you, facing the greatest apostasy the church has ever faced."

September 18, 1957, I received this communication.

"I have considered the matter to which you referred closed.

"I do not believe that you have the right to use the board minutes of the White Estate as you have done. The minutes are confidential and not intended for public use. I hope the time will never come when we take the position that men are to be condemned and disciplined because they come before properly constituted church boards to discuss questions that they may have pertaining to the work and belief of the church."

September 27, 1957, I answered:

"I thank you for your letter of September 18, wherein you state that 'the matter to which you refer is closed.' I called for an investigation. This you denied. You have condoned the men involved, and you have also said I had no right to use the information which has come to me, and then you closed the door. May I explain that the only way I have used my information is to inform you, and **no one else**. What else could I do? You state that if such information had come to you, you would not have used it. Quite an admission. I consider the present instance the greatest apostasy that has ever occurred in this denomination, and this you would have kept under cover! And now you have closed the door.... I do not believe, Brother Figuhr, that you have considered the seriousness of the situation. Our people will not stand for any tampering with, or attempt to tamper with the *Testimonies*. It will give them an uneasy feeling that all is not well at headquarters.

"Read again my letter of September 12. You can save the situation, but only as you are willing to open up the matter. You are about to ruin the denomination. I am praying for you."

My correspondence with Washington proceeded along this line until on December 16, 1957, I received this ultimatum: "They (the officers) therefore request that you cease your activities."

Three days later I received this additional word; "This will place you in plain opposition to your church, and will undoubtedly bring up the matter of your relationship to the church. In view of all this, the officers, as I have previously written, earnestly ask you to cease your activities."

Up till this time there had been no suggestion of a hearing. I was simply ordered to cease my activity, and the implied threat that if I did not do this, "it will undoubtedly bring up the matter of your relationship to the church." There was no suggestion of a hearing, I was simply ordered to stop my activity. I would be condemned without recourse. The threat that my name would come up for consideration could mean anything. There was no question raised as to the justice of my complaint. I was condemned already; the only question was what my punishment would be.

This brought to mind what had bean published in the *Eternity Extra*, that our men had "explained to Mr. Martin that they (the Adventists) had among their number certain members of their "lunatic fringe even as there are similar wild-eyed irresponsibles in every field of fundamental Christianity." In contrast to this lunatic fringe they had a "sane leadership," meaning themselves. I do not know how our leaders conducted themselves while with the evangelicals, but they left the impression upon these men that "the majority group of sane leadership (which) is determined to put the brakes on any members who seek to hold views divergent from that of the responsible leadership of the denomination." *Eternity Extra*, September, 1956, page 2.

Let the reader ponder this. We have a sane leadership according to their own estimation. We have also a lunatic fringe of wild-eyed irresponsibles. This sane leadership is determined to put the brakes on "any members who seek to hold views divergent from that of the responsible leadership of the denomination."

I could not believe this when I first read it. Here I was, for fifty years an honored member of the church, having held responsible positions. But if I dared hold "views divergent from that of the responsible leadership of the denomination," I became a member of the "wild-eyed irresponsibles" who constituted the "lunatic fringe" of the denomination; and without a hearing I was ordered to cease my activity or feel the "brakes" applied. If I did not now have the documents before me, I would have difficulty in believing that any "sane leadership" would attempt to stifle criticism and make threats against any members who seek to hold views divergent from that of the responsible leadership of the church. Had it come to this? Rome went but little further.

Some will object that this is only what the evangelicals say of our leaders. The fact remains that our men have never protested against these accusations. My own case makes clear that without any trial or hearing I was to be brought before the tribunal, not for a hearing, but to be condemned without a hearing by the men who had appointed themselves as judges. It is to be had in mind that this was before the General Conference of 1958, before the new theology had been officially accepted, and before the denomination had an opportunity to express itself on the subject. All public criticism must cease. If I did not cease, it will "undoubtedly bring up the matter of your relationship to the church." This was an ultimatum.

How did I react to this? As any man would. Here was an usurpation of authority. I wrote that I was a man of peace, and that I could be reasoned with, but not threatened. I felt, and I now feel, that this denomination is facing the apostasy foretold long ago, that our leaders are following the exact procedure which the Spirit of Prophecy outlined they would follow, and that I have a duty which I must not shirk. I regret very much that our leaders by their actions have made it possible for our enemies to bring deserved reproach to God's cause. In my early letters I mentioned again and again that our enemies would sooner or later discover our weakness and make capital of it. I pleaded with our leaders to make amends for what had been done; but without results. We are now reaping what we have sown.

In my next letter I shall recount the efforts I have made to get a hearing—not a secret hearing, but a public hearing—and if that was not thought best, a private hearing, but one that would be recorded and of which I would get a copy. In this I have failed. I shall give the documented reasons for my failure to get a recorded hearing.

I have been asked what I expect to accomplish. I have received hundreds of letters pledging support if I will only do certain things. I answer very few letters, as it is physically impossible for me to enter into correspondence. I have received many offers of advice and direction, but I don't want to involve others. I have had all manner of motives attributed to me, some good people apparently failing to understand that to attribute motives is judging. Also, it seems impossible for some to understand that doctrine in itself is important enough to furnish motive to protest. In this crisis we are now in, it would be cowardice for me to fail to come up to the help of the Lord against the mighty.

I have had three delegations come to me to plead with me to do something "practical." In effect they said: "We are with you, but you are not going at the matter in a practical way. The moment we take our stand with you, we may, and probably will, lose our position. (They were ministers.) If you had something to offer us, if you would start another movement which we could join, we would go with you. But to be left stranded without any prospect, is unrealistic. You will never get anywhere unless you have something to offer."

To that I answer that I am a Seventh-day Adventist, that I am not interested in starting any movement, and that I do not care for the support of any who hold such views. They are not the kind of material that will stand in the coming crisis.

I am a Seventh-day Adventist, rejoicing in the truth. Right and truth will triumph in the end. I am hoping that as the truth of the present situation becomes known, there will be men and women who will protest and exert influence enough to effect certain changes in our organization that will ensure men in holy office that are faithful to the truth once delivered to the saints.

I end this with hearty greeting to all. My next letter on the matter of a hearing should be an interesting one.

Till then, may the dear Lord be with you.

M. L. ANDREASEN
1911 Academy Place
Glendale 6, California

Dear Brother:

Thanks for your letter.
Let me assure you that I am in
good health — not a mental case,
not senile, not even dead, as has
been reported. But I am so busy
that I can not keep up with my
correspondence — I am all alone in
my work.

No, I have not recanted. The
denomination is departing from the
fundamentals. And I must protest.

And God still lives. So I am
of good courage.

Sincerely your brother,

M. L. Andreasen

Letter No. 5
WHY NOT A HEARING?

In a previous letter I have related how in the month of May, 1957, I came into possession of some official minutes of the White Board of Trustees—supposed to be secret which revealed an attempt to tamper with the *Testimonies* by having inserted in some of the volumes notes and explanations that would make it appear that Sr. White was in harmony with, or at least not opposed to, the new theology advocated in the *Ministry* and the book *Questions on Doctrine*. I was dumbfounded when I read this official document, and doubly perplexed when I learned that this plan had the sanction of the leadership, and was approved procedure. This would mean that men could freely attempt to have insertions made in the writings of the Spirit of Prophecy that would vitiate or change the intended meaning of what Sr. White had written. What assurance could we then have that the books being published were the unadulterated teachings of the author, and that they were not "remedied and corrected" as were other books, according to the account in the *Eternity Extra* of September, 1956?

While I felt uneasy at what the men had attempted to do, my real concern was the realization that this had been approved by the administration, and was henceforth to be accepted policy. Men could now go to the White Board, and with its approval, have inserted explanations and notes secretly and privately before any one would find out what was happening. And they could do this with the assurance that if any one learned of this and revealed what was being done, the administration would deal with such and threaten them unless they ceased their "activity."

In my case, I was told that the minutes were confidential, that I had no right to have them or even read them. Though I had quoted directly and correctly from the official minutes, I was told, "You are doing all this upon hearsay and upon confidential minutes which you have no right even to read." *Letter*, December, 1957. While the men wished to insert "notes," "explanations," "appendix notes," "foot notes," "suitable notes," "in future printings of the E. G. White writings," (note that all these statements are in the plural) the chairman minimized the matter by declaring in a letter of September 20, 1957, that all it involved was a "cross reference inserted at the bottom of a certain page;" that is, **one** cross reference, at the bottom of **one** page, in **one** of Sr. White's books. This is altogether at variance with the official record. How can this discrepancy be explained?

My first thought and hope was that I would be called to account immediately, and be asked to prove my charges or retract them; that an impartial group of men would be asked to conduct a hearing. But in this I was disappointed.

The first reaction to my "activity" came in a letter of December 16, 1957. There I was told: "The question of your activity was discussed by the officers of the General Conference and they deeply deplore what you are doing. They therefore request you to cease your present activities."

Before I had an opportunity to answer, I received the following on December 19:

> "I wish to repeat what I wrote you before, that men have a perfect right to go to boards, including the White Estate group, and make their suggestions without the fear of being disciplined or dealt with as heretics. When we recall that you are doing all this upon hearsay, and upon confidential minutes which you had no right even to read, it certainly impresses one as not the Adventist way of doing things. You were not present at this board meeting, and all you know about it is hearsay and the brief notes recorded by the secretary of that meeting. Now for you to go forward and broadcast a matter like this, certainly puts you in an unenviable light. If you do this, we shall have to do some broadcasting, too. This will again place you in plain opposition to your church, and will undoubtedly bring up the matter of your relationship to the church. In view of all this, the Officers as I have previously written, earnestly ask you to cease your activities."

As will be noted, there was no suggestion of a hearing to ascertain the truth or falsity of my charges. I was simply asked to cease my "activities," or else...

How did I react to this? As any man would under threat. I answered that I was a man of peace, that I could be reasoned with, but not threatened. I asked them to go ahead with their plans. I was ready for whatever might come.

What would come? I did not know what was meant by considering my "relationship to the church." It might mean anything. I know what impression they had left upon Dr. Barnhouse if any should object to their usurped authority. Here is what he recorded:

"The position of the Adventists seems to some of us in certain cases to be a new position; to them it may be merely the position of the majority group of sane leadership which is determined to put the brakes on any members who seek to hold views divergent from that of the responsible leadership of the denomination." *Eternity Extra*, September 1, 1956.

It seems unfortunate that our leaders should have left such an impression upon the evangelicals. This statement has now been in print three years. The attention of our leaders has been called to it and requests made that they disavow any such intention. But they have made no such disavowal or protest, and our people have somewhat reluctantly come to the conclusion that Mr. Barnhouse is correct in his estimate of our leaders. Add to this what Mr. Martin reports the leaders told him, that "they (the Adventists) have among their number certain members of their 'lunatic fringe' even as there are similar 'wild-eyed irresponsibles' in every field of fundamental Christianity." This is what our leaders told the evangelicals in discussing the important topic of the nature of Christ while in the flesh. These statements I consider an insult. It shows the contempt our leaders have for those who disagree with them. I think these statements are ample ground for impeachment. Our people are long-suffering, but this is the first time of which I know that insults are heaped upon loyal Seventh-day Adventists by the leaders.

A SHORT MEETING

The only meeting I have ever had with our leaders was one day in February, 1958, when two officers asked me to meet with them for the few minutes they had to spare between sessions of their business meetings. The chief thing seemed to be their desire to know if I intended to continue my "activity." I told them I would. A remark was made as to why I had not asked for a hearing. It had never occurred to me that I should **ask** for a hearing. I expected to be to be **summoned**. But thinking it over, the next day I wrote:

"I did not know that you wanted me to come to Washington for a hearing or discussion as you never mentioned such a thing. If that is your desire, I am ready to come. I have only one request, that the hearing be public, or that a stenographer be present, and that I receive a copy of the minutes." *Letter*, February 5, 1957.

In response to this I received this, dated February 10, inviting me to come, saying:

"In compliance with your wish, the brethren see no objection whatever in recording our conversation. It is suggested that a tape-recording would likely be the most practical way of doing this."

This was satisfactory to me. I noted, however, that nothing was said of my receiving a copy of the minutes. But perhaps, I thought, this was taken for granted, as I had made this a condition, and they had accepted my proposition. But I felt uneasy. If I should write for further confirmation it might appear that I was questioning their sincerity. But when by February 21, I had received no further word, I wrote:

"Whether by oversight or intent, you did not answer my request that I be given a copy of the minutes. This is necessary; for in any discussion of what is said or not said, it will be my word against that of twelve. I cannot afford to put myself in that position. This is the condition upon which I come."

To this I received a reply dated February 27:

"In the matter of record, I think I indicated in my letter of February 10 that the brethren had in mind recording on tape the proceedings of the meeting. This would provide a full record of what is said and done. We assume that such a complete record would be agreeable to you."

I had asked for a copy of the minutes, and this letter assured me that a tape recording would be made which would "provide a full record of what is said and done." It was assumed "that such a complete record would be agreeable to you." It would be. At last I was assured that a full and complete record would be made, and that according to their own suggestion it would be tape-recorded. I could ask for no more.

But having read *Questions on Doctrine* carefully, I had noticed that certain things would be said on one page, and a few pages further on this would be ignored. I had made note of certain double-tongued expressions, and it gave me a sense of uncertainty. I could not avoid the conviction that some of these expressions were used for the purpose of confusion and were intended to mislead.

I therefore reread the letters I had written, and also those I had received, especially the portions dealing with my request for a copy of the minutes. I found that nowhere had my request been acknowledged, but the issue had been avoided. This made me wonder. Had there throughout been a studied purpose **not** to give me a copy of the minutes, while the letters were so worded as to give the impression that I would get a copy? The evidence seemed to substantiate my suspicion. To make sure of my ground, I wrote on March 4 that I wanted absolute assurance, plainly stated, that I would get a "full and complete copy of the minutes" such as had been mentioned. I closed by saying: "On this point I must have absolute assurance."

As by March 12 I had received no answer, I wrote again, "I am still waiting for definite word that not only will a tape recording be made, but that I will get a copy. As I stated in my first letter, this is a necessary condition."

March 18 this answer came:

> "You have referred to a desire to have minutes kept, and also a copy of the minutes. In discussing this with the officers, it occurs to the brethren that we do this, which would seem fair to all concerned: a secretary be appointed from the group to write out the conclusions we arrive at, and these be submitted to the whole group for approval, after which each will be given a copy. We believe, Brother Andreasen, that this suggestion will be agreeable to you."

This was a wholly new and entirely different suggestion. After I had been told in the February 27th letter, that a tape-recording would be made, a "full" record of "what was said and done," and hope expressed that such "a complete record would be agreeable to me," I was now presented with a new and previously unheard of proposal, a complete face-about. There would be **no** stenographer, **no** tape-recording,

no minutes at all, but one of the men would write down the **conclusions** arrived at. And that was supposed to be agreeable to me! It certainly was not agreeable to me. It was a complete breach of faith. It was like substituting Leah for Rachel, a dishonorable transaction. I felt as did Jacob that I had been beguiled. Three weeks earlier, I had, been promised "a complete copy" of the **minutes** which it was hoped would be agreeable to me. Now I was offered a copy of the *conclusions*, which it was also hoped would be agreeable to me.

This March 18 letter reveals the fact that it was **never the intention** to give me a copy of the minutes, and yet they had played me along, thinking I would accept their suggestion, coming to a hearing or discussion, and having no record whatever of the discussion, but only of the **conclusions**. In the dark ages heretics were taken and convicted in secret. There was no habeas corpus act in existence then. And now the officers suggested an unrecorded session, where only a few would be present and no record of any kind be made! I consider this an immoral suggestion. Of what were they afraid? Moreover, before coming to such a hearing the condition was made "that you agree, in submitting your case to the General Conference committee, to abide by the decision of the committee." (*Letter* of May 13, 1958.) This clearly reveals the intent of the committee. A hearing is to be held, a secret hearing, and a discussion entered into, but before the hearing or discussion is held, I am to agree to accept their conclusion and verdict. Under these conditions, how could they help winning their case?

It appears that the officers had in mind appointing themselves accusers, jurors, judges, and executors. In a case involving points of doctrine where of necessity there must be discussion to arrive at sound conclusions, a neutral committee of men not directly involved in the controversy must hear the case. No judge ever hears a case where he is personally interested. He refuses to sit on a case where he is even remotely concerned. But our officers appoint themselves to hear the case and act as arbiters in a dispute involving points of theology, with powers to act, and ask that one side agree beforehand to accept whatever decision might be made. This, of course, is tantamount to accept the dictum of men elevated as administrators, executives, promoters, financiers, organizers and counselors to have jurisdiction over doctrine, for which work they are not educated. I have heard every one of them say, "I am no theologian."

March 26, 1958, I answered the letter which stated that there would
be no record of any kind, but that I would get a copy of the **conclusions**. I did not need this. I knew beforehand what they would be, for I
had already been judged and threatened. I had purposely been kept in
ignorance of the intent not to give me a copy of the minutes, but to try
me secretly. Apparently it was the intention to keep the matter from
becoming known, and if I agreed beforehand to accept their conclusions, I could be accused of breaking my promise if I made any further
comment. If I could be induced to come to Washington under these
conditions, I surely would be "sunk." With the whole case in mind,
with the repeated evasions of my request for a copy of the minutes, I
felt I had been deceived and ended my letter by saying, "Your broken
promise cancels the agreement." My faith in men had been severely
shaken.

April 3 I received an answer stating that my letter "had been received and its content presented to the officers." There was no mention whatever of my statement, "Your broken promise cancels the
agreement," the most important part. Also, this statement was not read
to the officers, for a month later I received a letter saying, "**Through
others** I have learned that you feel we have broken our promise to
you." This perversion of my words has gone out to the field, who
would naturally believe that I had written to **others** and not to the per-
son concerned. I don't do that kind of work.

In this same letter of April 3, the writer states:

> "It is true, as you state, that a tape recording was suggested
> at first, **without a promise, however, of giving you a
> copy**. Since making this suggestion, we have thought further
> about the matter and believe that such recording would not be
> a wise plan to follow.... A tape recording of every little remark
> would not be fair to the participants. In such discussions it is
> not uncommon for earnest men to make a slip which they later
> regret and correct. Mortal man is subject to such errors; but
> why preserve them? The sincere purpose of the meeting
> would be to arrive at conclusions together.... As I look over
> your letters, this would appear to be in accord with your
> original suggestion."

This makes clear several matters. It admits that a tape-recording
was suggested at first. It also makes clear that it was never the inten-

tion of giving me a copy, though the letters were written to hide this fact. It also states that the officers changed their mind and decided that it would not be a wise plan to record **anything**, as it "would not be fair to the participants," a most astounding reason, and revealing a most decided weakness. And then the last untrue statement: "As I look over your letters, this would appear to be **in accord with your original suggestion**."

Greater untruth was never uttered. I challenge the writer who says he looked over my letters to find any place where I say or intimate any such thing. And yet, this impression has gone to the field from Washington. Never suspecting that Washington would tell anything but the absolute truth, the men in the field who were admonished to "hold the line," naturally would believe that this was my "original suggestion" Nothing could be farther from the truth. Again and again, I stressed in all my letters that I wanted a copy of the **minutes**, and now the writer says as he looks over my letters that a copy of the **conclusions** was my original suggestion. What was his reason for such patent misstatement? I think I know. Is it possible that news from Washington is given a biased slant?

WHY THIS SUDDEN CHANGE?

There must have been some weighty reasons why it was suddenly decided not to have any record at all, after it was first decided to have a complete and full record "of all that was said and done?" The records of the 1888 crisis, the Alpha of apostasy, have largely disappeared, and the existing records are safely hidden and not available. We do not want a like situation in the time of the Omega. Let there be light.

I do not know why the change came about. I can only surmise. It was understood that my "activity" would be considered as well as my relationship to the church. The brethren also suggested that perhaps I had some matters also that should be discussed. I had. I made a list of these subjects. Here it is:

1. Elder Froom's articles, particularly those in the February number of the *Ministry,* 1957, downgrading Mrs. White.
2. The vault visits of Elders Anderson and Reed in regard to having insertions made in the writings of Mrs. White, and the general policies now prevailing.

3. A list of the topics discussed with the evangelicals which had taken "hundreds of hours," and the main conclusions reached.
4. A detailed list of the books "remedied and corrected" at the recommendation of Mr. Martin, and a further list of books yet to be remedied.
5. The $3,000 law suit.
6. Proselytization. What was agreed to?
7. The meaning of "putting the brakes on" and "lunatic fringe" and "wild-eyed irresponsibles."
8. The new university and the languishing foreign fields.
9. "Exchange monies."
10. A complete audit by a responsible firm of public accountants.

This list I did not send to Washington, for I well knew that it would be a matter of months to compass such a program. I suggested only a few subjects, and of course, I did know what the results would be. But, curiously enough, at just this time the brethren decided that it would not be wise to have any recording made. Under the circumstances I agree with the decision. The pusillanimous reason given for not having a record made—that the brethren might make remarks of which they later would repent—is simply inane. But let there be no misunderstanding. An accounting will yet have to be made.

To top it all comes this in the April 3 letter: "You never asked for a hearing." I will let the reader decide this question for himself. I answered:

> "Make no mistake on that point. I not only want a hearing, but such a hearing must be held if this sorry matter is ever to be settled. You say that you wonder if I am really sincere in wanting a hearing. Yes, I want a hearing. I demand one. Not a secret hearing. An open one, or else with a full and complete record of all that is said and done. This has been my desire from the beginning. No star chamber proceedings."

My last communication to headquarters was dated June 28, 1958. I asked if it was still the determination to give me a hearing with a tape-recording for me. A secretary answered:

"With reference to a tape-recording of the meeting, I am instructed to say that our correspondence reveals no promise of a tape recording for you. If desired, one can be made, but it will be kept in this office for a permanent record as previously stated."

This leaves me free. I have exhausted all means of corresponding with the men I should address. I can now speak to the church, as Christ said might be done if other means fail. This I shall do. But I still hold myself ready to come to a hearing or trial, properly conducted and properly recorded. Let the light in.

INHERITED PASSIONS

On page 383 of the book *Questions on Doctrine* occurs the statement that Christ "was exempt from the inherited passions and pollutions that corrupt the natural descendants of Adam."

This is not a quotation from the Spirit of Prophecy. It is a new doctrine that has never appeared in any Statement of Belief of the Seventh-day Adventist denomination, and is in direct conflict with our former statements of doctrine. It has not been "adopted by the General Conference in quadrennial session when accredited delegates from the whole field are present," as *Questions on Doctrine* says must be done if it is to be official. See page 3. It is therefore not approved or accepted doctrine.

TWO STATEMENTS

There are two statements in the *Testimonies* which are referred to as proving that Christ was exempt from inherited passions. The first says that Christ "is our example in all things. He is a brother in our infirmities, but not in possessing like passions." *Testimonies*, V. 2, p. 202. The other states, "He was a mighty petitioner, not possessing the passions of our human, fallen natures, but compassed with like infirmities, tempted in all points even as we are." *Ibid*. p. 509. Both of these statements mention passions, neither mentions pollutions. The word **exempt** is not found.

Does Sr. White's statement that Christ did not have or possess passions mean that He was **exempt** from them? No, for not to **have** passions is not equivalent to being **exempt** from them. They are two entirely different concepts. Exempt is defined "to free or excuse from some burdensome obligation; to take out, deliver, set free as from a rule which others must observe, which binds others; to be immune from." Was Christ excused from "a rule which others must observe, which binds others?" No, "God permitted His Son to come, a helpless babe, subject to (not exempt from) the weakness of humanity. He permitted Him to meet life's peril in common with every human soul, to fight the battle as every child of humanity must fight it, at the risk of failure and eternal loss." *Desire of Ages* p. 49. "While He was a child, He thought and spoke as a child, but no trace of sin marred the image of God within Him. Yet He was not exempt from temptation. He was subject to (not exempt from) all the conflicts which we have to meet." *Ibid.* p. 71. "God spared not His own Son." (Romans 8:32). "No child of humanity will ever be called to live a holy life amid so fierce a conflict with temptation as was our Saviour." *Desire of Ages*, p. 71. "It was necessary for Him to be constantly on guard to preserve His purity." *Ibid.* A man may not **have** cancer, but does that mean that he is **immune** from it, **exempt** from it? Not at all. Next year he may be afflicted with it. Sr. White does not say that Christ was **exempt** from passions. She says He did not **have** passions, did not **possess** passions, not that He was immune from them.

Why did Christ not have passions? Because "the soul must **purpose** the sinful act before passion can dominate over reason, or iniquity triumph over conscience." *Testimonies*, V. 5, p. 177. And Christ did not **purpose** any sinful act. Not for a moment was there in Him a sinful propensity. He was pure, holy, undefiled. But this did not mean that He was exempt from temptation or sin. "He could have sinned, He could have fallen." *Bible Commentary*, V. 5, p. 1128. I am still puzzled how anyone can make Sr. White say that Christ was exempt, when she says just the opposite, and does not use the word exempt.

IS TEMPTATION SIN?

Temptation is not sin; but it may become so if we yield to it. "When impure thoughts are **cherished**, they need not be expressed in word or act to consummate the sin and bring the soul into condemnation." *Testimonies*, V. 4, p. 623. "An impure thought **tolerated**, an unholy desire cherished, and the soul is contaminated... Every unholy thought must be instantly repelled." *Testimonies*, V. 5, p. 177.

Satan tempts us to get us to sin. God uses **controlled** temptation to strengthen us and teach us to resist. Satan tempted Adam in the garden; he tempted Abraham and all the prophets; he tempted Christ; he tempts all men, but God will "not suffer you to be tempted above that ye are able." (1 Corinthians 10:13).

"Christ was a free moral agent who could have sinned had He so desired. He was at liberty to yield to Satan's temptations and work at cross purposes with God. If this were not so, if it had not been possible for Him to fall, He could not have been tempted in all points as the human family is tempted." *Youths' Instructor*, October 26, 1899.

THE GREAT LAW OF HEREDITY

Questions on Doctrine says, page 383, that Christ was "exempt from the inherited passions and pollutions that corrupt the natural descendants of Adam." Every child that is born into this world inherits varying traits from his ancestors. Did Christ likewise inherit such traits? Or was He exempt? Here is the answer:

"Like every child of Adam He accepted the results of the working of the great law of heredity." *Desire of Ages*, p. 48. "What these results were is shown in the history of His earthly ancestors." *Ibid*. Some of these ancestors were good people; some were not so good; some were bad; some were very bad. There were thieves, murderers, adulterers, deceivers, among them. He had the same ancestors that all of us have. "He came with **such** a heredity to share our sorrows and temptations." *Ibid*. "Jesus **accepted** humanity when the race had been weakened by four thousand years of sin." *Ibid*.

In view of these and many other statements, how can any say that He was **exempt**? Far from being exempt or reluctantly **submitting** to these conditions, He **accepted** them. Twice this is stated in the quotations here made. He accepted the results of the working of the great law of heredity, and with "such heredity He came to share our sorrows and temptations."

The choice of the devout Adventist is therefore between *Questions on Doctrine* and *Desire of Ages*, between falsehood and truth. "God permitted His Son to come, a helpless babe, subject to the weakness of humanity. He permitted Him to meet life's peril in common with every human soul, to fight the battle as every child of humanity must fight it, at the risk of failure and eternal loss." *Desire of Ages*, p. 49. "Christ knew that the enemy would come to every human being to take advantage of weakness…and by passing over the ground which man must travel, our Lord has prepared the way for us to overcome." *Desire of Ages*, p. 122, 123. "Upon Him who had laid off His glory, and **accepted** the hereditary weakness of humanity, the redemption of the world must rest." *Ibid*. p. 11.

Few, even of our ministers, know anything of what Sr. White calls the great law of heredity. Yet this is the law which made the incarnation effective and made Christ a real man, like one of us in all things. That Christ should be like one of us in all things, Paul considered a moral necessity on the part of God, and makes bold so to state. Says he: "In all things it **behooved** him to be made like unto his brethren, that he might be a merciful and faithful high priest in things pertaining to God to make reconciliation for the sins of the people; for in that he himself hath suffered, being tempted, he is able to succor them that are tempted." (Hebrews 2:17,18). **Behooved** here means "ought to," a moral duty devolving upon God.

The great law of heredity was decreed by God to make salvation possible, and is one of the elemental laws that has never been abrogated. Take that law away, and we have no Saviour that can be of help or example to us. Graciously Christ "accepted" this law, and thus made salvation possible. To teach that Christ was **exempt** from this law negates Christianity and makes the incarnation a pious hoax. May God deliver Seventh-day Adventists from such teaching and teachers!

POLLUTION

I have not touched upon the subject of pollution, though it is mentioned in *Questions on Doctrine* in connection with passions. Christ was subject to the great law of heredity, but that has nothing to do with pollution. Impure thoughts tolerated, unholy desires cherished, evil passions indulged in, will issue in contamination, pollution, and downright sin. But Christ was not affected by any of this. He "received no defilement;" "Jesus, coming to dwell in humanity, received no pollution." *Desire of Ages*, p. 266.

Passion and pollution are two different things, and should not be placed together as they are in *Questions on Doctrine*. Passion can generally be equated with temptation, and as such is not sin. An impure thought may come unbidden even on a sacred occasion, but it will not defile; it is not sin, unless it is dwelt upon and tolerated. An unholy desire may suddenly flash to mind at Satan's instigation; but it is not sin unless it is cherished

The law of heredity applies to passions and not to pollutions. If pollution is hereditary, then Christ would have been polluted when He came to this world and could not therefore be "that holy thing." (Luke 1:35). Even the children of an unbelieving husband are called holy, a statement that should be a comfort to the wives of such husbands. (1

Corinthians 7:14). As Adventists, however, we do not believe in original sin.

Of this matter of pollution there is much to say. But as the problem we are facing deals only with passions, we shall not discuss pollutions further. On occasion I may have more to say about passions, for I consider the statement in *Question on Doctrine* deadly heresy, destructive of the atonement.

My next letter will be the last one in this series. But if the reader will consult the list of ten subjects which I have enumerated elsewhere in this letter, he will see that there is yet much to be done. And that list is not exhaustive. However, I shall give time for what I have said to sink in, for large bodies move slowly, and it takes time for the leaven to "leaven the whole lump." But the leaven is working, and in due time expected results will come. But I am in no haste. Time is with truth, and truth will make its way, and is not dependent on any human instrument. I get many encouraging letters, and am thankful for them, and only sorry that I must leave most of them unanswered. One rather prominent man from Washington wrote me of the confusion existing there, and stated: "We are watching events, and when the time comes, we will be ready to act. Personally, I do not believe that the time is quite ripe, but nearly so. We are with you, and you can depend on us."

I am glad to report that my health is good, and that I am enjoying life to the limit. It is wonderful to live in such a time as this. "I am immortal till my work is done." That may be tomorrow, but if so, I am satisfied and ready.

Greetings to all my friends with 1 Thessalonians 5:25.

Letter No. 6

THE ATONEMENT

The serious student of the atonement is likely to be perplexed when he consults the Spirit of Prophecy to find two sets of apparently contradictory statements in regard to the atonement. He will find that when Christ "offered Himself on the cross, a perfect atonement was made for the sins of the people." *Signs of the Times*, June 28, 1899. He will find that the Father bowed before the cross "in recognition of its perfection. 'It is enough,' He said, 'the atonement is complete.' " *Review and Herald*, September 24, 1901.

But in *Great Controversy* he will find this: "At the conclusion of the 2300 days, in 1844, Christ entered the most holy place of the heavenly sanctuary, to perform the **closing** work of the atonement." p. 422. In *Patriarchs and Prophets* p. 357, I read that sins will "stand on record in the sanctuary until the final atonement." (in 1844) Page 358 states that in "the **final** atonement the sins of the truly penitent are to be blotted from the records of Heaven." *Early Writings*, page 253, says that "Jesus entered the most holy of the heavenly at the end of the 2300 days of Daniel 8, to make the **final** atonement."

The first set of statements says that the atonement was made on the cross; the other says that the **final** atonement was made 1800 years later. I have found seven statements that the atonement was made on the cross; I have twenty-two statements that the final atonement was made in Heaven. Both of these figures are doubtless incomplete; for there may be others that have escaped my attention. It is evident, however, that I may not accept one set of statements and reject the other if I wish to arrive at truth. The question therefore is which statements are true? Which are false? Or, are both true? If so, how can they be harmonized?

I was perplexed when in the February number of the *Ministry*, 1957, I found the statement that "the sacrificial act of the cross (was) a complete, perfect, and **final** atonement." This was in distinct contradiction to Mrs. White's pronouncement that the **final** atonement began in 1844. I thought that this might be a misprint, and wrote to Washington calling attention to the matter, but found it was not a misprint but an official and approved statement. If we still hold the Spirit of Prophecy as of authority, we therefore have two contradictory beliefs: the final atonement was made at the cross; the final atonement began in 1844.

DEFINITION OF ATONEMENT

I have listened to several discussions of the meaning of the Hebrew word "kaphar," which is the word used in the original for atonement, but have received little help. The best definition I have found is a short explanatory phrase in *Patriarchs and Prophets, p.* 358, which simply states that the atonement, "the great work of Christ, or **blotting out of sin**, was represented by the services on the day of atonement." This definition is in harmony with Leviticus 16:30 which says that "the priest shall make an atonement for you, to **cleanse** you, that ye may be **clean from all your sins** before the Lord." Atonement is here equated with being "clean from all your sins." As sin was the cause of separation between God and man, the removing of sin would again unite God and man. And this would be at-one-ment.

Christ did not need any atonement, for He and the Father were always one. (John 10:30). Christ prayed for His disciples "that they may all be one, as thou, Father, art in me and I in thee, that they also may be one in us." (John 17:21).

The definition of **atonement** as consisting of three words—at-one-ment— is by some considered obsolete, but it nevertheless represents vital truth. Mrs. White thus uses it. Says she: "unless they accept the atonement provided for them in the remedial sacrifice of Jesus Christ who is our atonement, at-one-ment, with God." *MS.* 122, 1901.

God's plan is that in "the fullness of time he might gather together in **one** all things in Christ." (Ephesians 1:10). When this is done, the family of Heaven and the family of earth are one." *Desire of Ages*, p. 835. Then "one pulse of harmony and gladness beats through the vast creation." *Great Controversy*, p. 678. At last the atonement is complete.

TWO PHASES OF THE ATONEMENT

Much confusion in regard to the atonement arises from a neglect to recognize the two divisions of the atonement. Note what is said of John the Baptist, "He did not distinguish clearly the two phases of Christ's work—as a suffering sacrifice, and a conquering king." *Desire of Ages*, pp. 136,137. The book *Questions on Doctrine* makes the same mistake. It does not distinguish clearly; in fact it does not distinguish at all; it does not seem to **know** of the two phases; hence the confusion.

THE FIRST PHASE

The first phase of Christ's atonement was that of a suffering sacrifice. This began before the world was, included the incarnation, Christ's life on earth, the temptation in the wilderness, Gethsemane, Golgotha, and ended when God's voice called Christ from the "stony prison house of death." The fifty third chapter of Isaiah is a vivid picture of this.

Satan had overcome Adam in the garden of Eden, and in a short time nearly the whole world had come under his sway. At the time of Noah there were only eight souls who entered the ark. Satan claimed to be prince of this world, and no one had challenged him.

But God did not recognize Satan's claim to dominion, and when Christ came to earth, the Father "gave the world into the hands of the Son, that through His mediatorial work He may completely vindicate the holiness and the binding claims of every precept of the divine law." *Bible Echo*, January, 1887. This was a challenge to Satan's claim, and thus began in earnest the great controversy between Christ and Satan.

> "Christ took the place of fallen Adam. With the sins of the world laid upon Him, He would go over the ground where Adam stumbled." *Review and Herald*, February 24, 1874. "Jesus volunteered to meet the highest claims of the law." *Ibid.* September 2, 1890. "Christ made Himself responsible for every man and woman on earth." *Ibid.,* February 27, 1900.

As Satan claimed ownership of the earth, it was necessary for Christ to overcome Satan before He could take possession of His kingdom. Satan knew this, and hence made an attempt to kill Christ as soon as He was born. However, as a contest between Satan and a helpless child in a manger, would not be fair, God frustrated this.

The first real encounter between Christ and Satan took place in the wilderness. After forty days of fasting Christ was weak and emaciated, at death's door. At this time Satan made his attack. But Christ resisted, even "unto blood," and Satan was compelled to retire defeated. But he did not give up. Throughout Christ's ministry, Satan dogged His footsteps, and made every moment a hard battle.

GETHSEMANE

The climax of Christ's struggle with Satan, came in the garden of Gethsemane. Hitherto Christ had been upheld by the knowledge of the approval of the Father. But now He "was overpowered by the terrible fear that God was removing His presence from Him." *Spirit of Prophecy*, Vol. 3, p. 95. If God should forsake Him, could He still resist Satan and die rather than yield? "Three times His humanity shrank from the last, crowning sacrifice...The fate of humanity trembled in the balance." *Ibid.*, p. 99. "As the Father's presence was withdrawn, they saw Him sorrowful with a bitterness of sorrow exceeding that of the last struggle with death." *Desire of Ages*, p. 759. "He fell dying to the ground," but with His last ounce of strength murmured, 'If this cup may not pass from me except I drink it, Thy will be done'...A heavenly peace rested upon His bloodstained face. He had borne that which no human being could ever bear; He had tasted the sufferings of death for every man." *Desire of Ages*, p. 694. In His death, He was victor.

"When Christ said, 'It is finished,' God responded, 'It is finished, the human race shall have another trial.' The redemption price is paid, and Satan fell like lightning from Heaven." *MS.* 11, 1897.

"As the Father beheld the cross He was satisfied. He said, It is enough, the offering is complete." *Signs of the Times*. September 30, 1899. It was necessary, however, that there should be given the world a stern manifestation of the wrath of God, and so, "in the grave Christ was the captive of divine justice." *M.V.F.* February 24, 1898. It must be abundantly attested that Christ's death was real, so He must "remain in the grave the allotted period of time." *Review and Herald*, April 26, 1898. When the time was expired, a "messenger was sent to relieve the Son of God from the debt for which He had become responsible, and for which He had made full atonement." *MS.*, 94, 1897.

"In the intercessory prayer of Jesus with His Father, He claimed that He had fulfilled the conditions which made it obligatory upon the Father to fulfill His part of the contract made in Heaven with regard to fallen man. He prayed, "I have finished the work which Thou gavest me to do." Mrs. White then makes this explanation, "That is, He had wrought out a righteous character on earth as an example for men to follow." *Spirit of Prophecy*, Vol. 3, p. 260.

The "contract" between the Father and the Son made in Heaven, included the following: 1. The Son was to work out a "righteous character on earth as an example for man to follow." 2. Not only was Christ to work out such a character, but He was to demonstrate that man also could do this; and thus man would become "more precious than fine gold, even a man than the golden wedge of Ophir." 3. If Christ thus could present man as a new creature in Christ Jesus, then God was to "receive repentant and obedient men, and would love them even as He loves His Son." *Spirit of Prophecy*, Vol. 3, p. 260; *Desire of Ages,* 790.

Christ had "fulfilled **one phase** of His priesthood by dying on the cross. He is now fulfilling **another phase** by pleading before the Father the case of repenting, believing sinners, presenting to God the offerings of His people." *MS.* 42 1901. "In His incarnation He had reached the prescribed limit **as a sacrifice**, but not as a redeemer." *MS.* III, 1897. On Golgotha He was the victim, the sacrifice. That was as far as He could go as a sacrifice. But now His work as **redeemer** began. "When Christ cried 'It is finished,' God's unseen hand rent the strong fabric which composed the veil of the temple from top to bottom. The way into the holiest of all was made manifest." *Ibid.*

With the cross the **first phase** of Christ's work as the " suffering sacrifice" ended. He had gone the "prescribed limit" as a **sacrifice**. He had finished His work "thus far." And now, with the Father's approval of the sacrifice, He was empowered to be the Saviour of mankind. At the ensuing coronation forty days later He was given all power in Heaven and earth, and officially installed as High Priest.

THE SECOND PHASE

"**After** His ascension our Saviour **began** His work as High Priest… In harmony with the typical service He began His ministration in the holy place, and at the termination of the prophetic days in 1844… He entered the most holy to perform the last division of His solemn work, to cleanse the sanctuary." *Spirit of Prophecy*, Vol. 4, pp. 265, 266. On the same page, 266, Sr. White repeats, apparently for emphasis, "at the termination of the 2300 days in 1844, Christ then entered the most holy place of the heavenly sanctuary, into the presence of God, to perform the **closing** work of atonement preparatory to His coming." The reader cannot fail to note how clearly and emphatically this is stated. John the Baptist "did not distinguish clearly the two phases of Christ's work, as a suffering sacrifice and a conquering king." *Desire of Ages*, pp. 136, 137. Our theologians are making the same mistake today—and are inexcusable. They have light which John did not have.

In studying this part of the atonement, we are entering a field that is distinctly Adventist, and in which we differ from all other denominations. This is our unique contribution to religion and theology, that which "has made us a separate people, and has given character and power to our work." *Counsels to Editors and Writers*, p. 54. In the same place she warns us against making "void the truths of the atonement, and destroy our confidence in the doctrines which we have held sacred since the third angel's message was first given."

This is vital counsel, and written for this very time when efforts are being made by some among us to have others believe that we are like the churches about us, an evangelical body and not a sect. Paul, in his day, had the same heresy to meet. He was accused of being a "pestilent fellow," "a ringleader of the sect of the Nazarenes." (Acts 24:5). In his answer before Felix, Paul confessed that after the "way which **they call a sect**, so serve I the God of our Fathers believing all things which are according to the law and which are written in the prophets." (Acts 24:14. R. V.) In those days men spoke sneeringly of the true church as a sect, as men do now. Paul was not disturbed by this. We have no record that he attempted to have the church of the living God recognized as an evangelical body by men who trampled the law of God in the dust. On the contrary, whatever they might call him and his "sect," he confessed that he believed "all things which are written in the law and the prophets." (Verse 14).

The religious journal, *Christianity Today*, states in the March 3, 1958 issue, that "the Adventists today are contending vigorously that they are truly evangelical. They appear to want to be so regarded." Mentioning the book, *Questions on Doctrine*, it says that this "is the Adventist answer to the question whether it ought to be thought of as a sect or a fellow evangelical denomination." It states further that "the book" is published in an effort to convince the religious world that we **are** evangelical and one of them.

This is a most interesting and dangerous situation. As one official who was not in favor of what was being done stated to me: "We are being sold down the river." What a sight for Heaven and earth! The church of the living God which has been given the commission to preach the gospel to every creature under Heaven and call men to come out of Babylon, is now standing at the door of these churches asking permission to enter and become one of them. How are the mighty fallen! Had their plan succeeded, we might now be a member of some evangelical association and not a distinctive Seventh-day Adventist church anymore, in secrecy "sold down the river." This is more than apostasy. This is giving up Adventism. It is the rape of a whole people. It is denying God's leading in the past. It is the fulfillment of what the Spirit of Prophecy said years ago:

"The enemy of souls has sought to bring in the supposition that a great reformation was to take place among Seventh-day Adventists, and that this reformation would consist in **giving up the doctrines** which stand as pillars of our faith, and engaging in a process of reorganization. Were this reformation to take place, what would result? The principles of truth that God in His wisdom has given to the remnant church would be discarded. **Our religion would be changed.** The fundamental principles that have sustained the work for the last fifty years would be accounted an error. A new organization would be established. Books of a new order would be written. A system of intellectual philosophy would be introduced... Nothing would be allowed to stand in the way of the new movement." *Series B, No. 2*, pp. 54, 55.

"Be not deceived; many will depart from the faith, giving heed to seducing spirits and doctrines of devils. We have before us the alpha of this danger. The omega will be of a most startling nature." *Ibid*. p. 16.

"When men standing in the position of leaders and teachers work under the power of spiritualistic ideas and sophistries, shall we keep silent for fear of injuring their influence, while souls are being beguiled?...Those who feel so very peaceable in regard to the works of the men who are spoiling the faith of the people of God, are guided by a delusive sentiment." *Ibid*, pp. 9, 11.

"Renewed energy is now needed. Vigilant action is called for. Indifference and sloth will result in the loss of personal religion and of Heaven...My message to you is: No longer consent to listen without protest to the perversion of truth. We must firmly refuse to be drawn away from the platform of eternal truth, which since 1844 has stood the test." *Ibid*. pp. 14, 15, 50.

"I hesitated and delayed about the sending out of that which the Spirit of the Lord impelled me to write. I did not want to be compelled to present the misleading influence of these sophistries. But in the providence of God, the errors that have been coming in **must be met**." *Ibid*. p. 55.

"What influence is it that would lead men at this stage of our history to work in an **underhanded**, powerful way to tear down the foundation of our faith—the foundation that was laid at the beginning of our work by prayerful study of the word and by revelation? Upon this foundation we have been building the past fifty years. Do you wonder that when I see the beginning of a work that would remove some of the pillars of our faith, I have something to say? I must obey the command, 'Meet it.' *Ibid*. p. 58.

All this was written to meet the apostasy in the alpha period. We are now in the omega period which Sr. White said would come, and which would be of a "startling nature." And the words are even more applicable now than then. Is the reader one of "those who feel so very peaceable in regard to the works of the men who are spoiling the faith of the people of God?" *Ibid*. p. 11. "Shall we keep silent for fear of injuring their influence, while souls are being beguiled?" *Ibid*. p. 9. It is time to stand up and be counted. There are times when I have been tempted to think that I stood alone as did Elijah. But God told him that there were 7000 others. There are more than that now, thank God. They need to reveal themselves—and they are doing it. Most heartening are the letters I am receiving. It is with deep regret that I find I am unable to enter into extended correspondence. I am overwhelmed with work.

Christ's death on the cross corresponds to the moment when on the day of atonement the high priest had just killed the Lord's goat in the court. The death of the goat was necessary, for without its blood there could be no atonement. But the death in and of itself was not the atonement, though it was the first and necessary step. Sr. White speaks of the "atonement **commenced** on earth." *Spirit of Prophecy*, Vol. 3, p. 261. Says Scripture: "It is the **blood** that maketh atonement." (Leviticus 17:11). And, of course, there could be no blood until after the death had taken place. Without a blood ministration the people would be in the same position as those who on the Passover slew the lamb but failed to place the blood on the door posts. "When I see the **blood**," said God, "I will pass over you." (Exodus 12: 13). The death was useless without the ministration of the blood. It was the blood that counted.

It is the blood that is to be applied, not "an act," "a great act," "a sacrificial act," "an atoning act," "the act of the cross," "the benefits of the act of the cross," "the benefits of the atonement," all of which expressions are used in *Questions on Doctrine*, but any reference to the blood is carefully avoided. It is not an act of any kind that is to be applied. It is the **blood**. Yet in all the 100 pages in the book dealing with the atonement, not once is the blood spoken of as being applied, or ministered. Can this be merely an oversight, or is it intended? Are we teaching a bloodless atonement? Elder Nichols states the Adventist position correctly when he says, "We believe that Christ's work of atonement was **begun** rather than **completed** on Calvary." *Answers to Objections*, p. 408. This was published in 1952. We shall be interested to see what the new edition will say. Many are waiting to find out what they are to believe on this important question.

BLOOD ATONEMENT

Here are some expressions from the Spirit of Prophecy in regard to blood atonement:

"Jesus was clothed with priestly garments. He gazed in pity on the remnant, and with a voice of deep pity cried, 'My **blood**, Father; My **blood**; My **blood**; My **blood**.' " *Early Writings*, p. 38.

"He appears in the presence of God as our great High Priest, ready to accept the repentance, and to answer the prayers of His people, and, through the merits of His own righteousness, to present them to the Father. He raises His wounded hands to God, and claims their **bloodbought pardon**. I have graven them on the palms of my hands, He pleads. Those **memorial wounds** of my humiliation and anguish **secure to my church** the best gifts of omnipotence." *Spirit of Prophecy*, Vol. 3, pp. 261, 262.

"The ark that enshrines the tables of the law is covered with the mercy seat, before which Christ pleads His **blood** in the sinner's behalf." *Great Controversy*, p. 415.

"When in the typical service the high priest left the holy place on the day of atonement, He went in before God to present the blood of the sin-offering, in behalf of all Israel who truly repented of their sins. So Christ had only completed one part of His work as our intercessor, to enter upon another portion of the work, and He still **pleaded His blood** before the Father in behalf of sinners." *Ibid*. p. 429.

Christ is "now officiating before the ark of God, **pleading His blood** in behalf of sinners." *Ibid*. p. 433.

"Christ, the great high priest, **pleading His blood** before the Father in the sinner's behalf, bears upon His heart the name of every repentant, believing soul." *Patriarchs and Prophets*, p. 351.

"As Christ at His ascension appeared in the presence of God to **plead His blood** in behalf of penitent believers, so the priest in the daily ministration sprinkled the blood of the sacrifice in the holy place in the sinner's behalf." *Patriarchs and Prophets*, p. 357.

"The **blood of Christ**, while it was to release the repentant sinner from the condemnation of the law, was not to cancel the sin; it was to stand on record in the sanctuary until the final atonement." *Patriarchs and Prophets,* p. 357.

And with all these statements before him, not once does the author of *Questions on Doctrine* mention the blood as being applied or minis-tered.

THE FINAL ATONEMENT

"The Father ratified the covenant made with Christ, that He would receive repentant and obedient men, and would love them even as He loves His Son." This, as stated above, was on the condition that "Christ was to complete His work and fulfill His pledge to make a man more precious than fine gold, even a man than the golden wedge of Ophir." *Desire of Ages*, in 790. "This Christ guarantees." *Spirit of Prophecy*, Vol. 3, p. 250.

When Christ says in His high priestly prayer, "I have finished the work which Thou gavest me to do," (John 17:4) Sr. White comments: "He had wrought out a righteous character on earth as an example for man to follow." *Spirit of Prophecy*, Vol. 3, p. 260.

In working out this righteous character, Christ demonstrated that it could be done. But could others do the same? That needed to be demonstrated also. Christ had **guaranteed** it could. It was now for Christ to make good His pledge.

Character is not created. It is **made**; it is **developed**; it is **built** through manifold tests and temptations and trials. God at first gives a light test, then a little stronger, and still a little stronger. Little by little resistance to temptations grows stronger, and after a while certain temptations cease to be temptations. A man may have a great struggle with tobacco; but at last he is victorious, and his victory may be so complete that tobacco is a temptation no longer.

Thus, ideally, it should be with every temptation. Holiness is not attained in a day. "Redemption is that **process** by which the soul is trained for Heaven." *Desire of Ages*, p. 330. A man may gain victories every day, but still may not have attained. Even Paul had to admit that he had not "already attained, either already perfect." But undaunted exclaims, "I follow after that I may apprehend that for which also I am apprehended of Jesus Christ." (Philippians 3:12).

Christ had pledged to make man "finer than gold," even the golden wedge of Ophir. In this work man must not be a submissive instrument only; he must take an active part. Note these quotations:

"The ransom of the human race was appointed to give man another trial." *MS.*, 14, 1898. "The plan of salvation was designed to redeem the fallen race, to give man another trial." *Signs of the Times*, April 26, 1899. God "looked upon the victim expiring on the cross and said, 'It is finished; the human race shall have **another trial**.' " *Youth's Instructor*, June 21, 1900. "That the transgressor might have **another trial** the eternal Son of God interposed Himself to bear the punishment of transgression." *Review and Herald*, February 8, 1898. "He suffered in our stead that men could have **another test and trial**." *Special Instruction Relating to the Review and Herald Office*, p. 28. "As Jesus was accepted as our substitute and surety, every one of us will be accepted if we stand the test and trial **for ourselves**" *Review and Herald*, June 10, 1890. "The Saviour overcame to show man how he may overcome." "**Man must work with his human power** aided by the divine power of Christ, to resist and to conquer **at any cost to himself**. In short, he must **overcome as Christ overcame**.... Man must do his part; he must be victor on his own account, through the strength and grace that Christ gives him." *Testimonies*, Vol. 4, p. 32, 33.

Christ had pledged to make men overcomers; he had **"guaranteed"** this. It was no easy task; but the work of atonement was not finished until and unless He did it. And so Christ persevered till His task should be done. Out of the last generation, out of the weakest of the weak, Christ selects a group with which to make the demonstration that man can **overcome as Christ overcame**. In the 144,000 Christ will stand justified and glorified. They prove that it is possible for man to live a life pleasing to God under all conditions, and that men can at last stand "in the sight of a holy God without an intercessor." *Great Controversy*, p. 614. The testimony is given them, "they have stood without an intercessor through the final outpouring of God's judgments." *Great Controversy*, p. 649. "They are the chosen ones, joint heirs with Christ in the great firm of Heaven. **They overcame, as He overcame**." *MS*. November 28, 1897. To us comes the invitation, "Now, while our High Priest is making atonement for us, we should seek to become perfect in Christ." *Great Controversy*, p. 623.

A MYSTERY

In his epistle to the Ephesians, Paul presents us with a mystery. Says he, "For this cause shall a man leave his father and his mother and shall be joined unto his wife, and the two shall be one flesh. This is a great mystery; but I speak concerning Christ and the church." (Ephesians 5: 31, 32). Marriage fitly represents the union between Christ and the church, effected by the atonement. In harmony with this picture of a marriage, the public announcement is made at the close of probation: "The marriage of the Lamb is come, and His wife has made herself ready... And to her it was granted that she should be arrayed in linen, clean and white; for the linen is the righteousness of the saints." (Revelation 19:8). As husband and wife are one, so now are Christ and the church. The atonement, the true atonement, the final atonement, the complete atonement, has been made. "The family of Heaven and the family of earth are one." *Desire of Ages*, p. 835.

THE 144,000

Practically all Adventists have read the last few chapters in *Great Controversy*, which describe the fearful struggle through which God's people will pass before the end. As Christ was tried to the utmost in the temptation in the wilderness and in the garden of Gethsemane, so the 144,000 will likewise be tried. They will apparently be left to perish, as their prayers remain unanswered as were Christ's in Gethsemane when His petitions were denied. But their faith will not fail. With Job they exclaim, "Though He slay me, yet will I trust Him." (Job 13:15).

The final demonstration of what God can do in humanity is made in the last generation who bears all the infirmities and weaknesses which the race has acquired through six thousand years of sin and transgression. In the words of Sr. White they bore "the results of the working of the **great law of heredity**," *Desire of Ages*, p. 48. The **weakest** of mankind are to be subjected to the **strongest** of Satan's temptations, that the power of God might be abundantly shown. "It was an hour of fearful, terrible agony to the saints. Day and night they cried unto God for deliverance. To outward appearance, there was no possibility of their escape." *Early Writings*, p. 283.

According to the new theology which our leaders have accepted and are now teaching, the 144,000 will be subjected to a temptation immeasurably stronger than any Christ ever experienced. For while the last generation will bear the weaknesses and passions of their forefathers, they claim that Christ was exempt from all these. Christ, we are told, did not inherit any of the passions "that corrupt the natural descendants of Adam." *Questions on Doctrine*, p. 383. He was therefore functioning on a higher and altogether different level from men who have to battle with inherited passions and hence He does not know and has not experienced the real power of sin. But this is not the kind of savior I need. I need One who has been **tempted in all points like as we are**." (Hebrews 4:15). The "substitute Christ" which our leaders present to us, I must reject and do reject. Thank God, "we have not a high priest which cannot be touched with the feeling of our infirmities, but was in all points tempted like as we are, yet without sin." (Ibid).

INDICTMENT AGAINST GOD

But more than even this is involved in the new theology; it places an indictment against God as the author of a scheme to deceive both men and Satan. Here is the situation:

Satan has consistently maintained that God is unjust in requiring men to obey His law, which he claims is impossible. God has maintained that it **can** be done, and to substantiate His claim offered to send His Son to this world to prove His contention. The Son did come and kept the law and challenged men to convince Him of sin. He was found to be sinless, holy and without blame. He proved that the law could be kept, and God stood vindicated; and His requirement that men keep His commandments—was found to be just. God had won, and Satan was defeated.

But there was a hitch in this; for Satan claimed that God had not played fair; He had favored His Son, had "exempted" Him from the results of the working of the great law of heredity to which all other men were subject; He had exempted Christ "from the inherited passions and pollutions that corrupt the natural descendants of Adam." *Questions on Doctrine,* p. 383. He had not exempted mankind in general, but Christ only. That, of course, invalidated Christ's work on earth. He was no longer one of us who had demonstrated the power of God to keep men from sinning. He was a deceiver whom God had given preferred treatment and was not afflicted with inherited passions as men are.

Satan had little difficulty in having men accept this view; the Catholic church accepted it; in due time, the evangelicals gave their consent; and in 1956 the leaders of the Adventist church also adopted this view. It was the matter of "exemption" that caused Peter to take Christ aside and say, "Be it far from thee, Lord; this shall not be unto thee," which so raised the wrath of Christ that He told Peter, "Get thee behind me, Satan." (Matthew 16:22, 23). Christ did not want to be exempt. He told Peter, "Thou savourest not the things that be of God." So some today savour not the things of God. They think it merely a matter of semantics. God pity such and open their eyes to the things that be of God. With the surrender of the Adventist leaders to the monstrous doctrine of an "exempt" Christ, Satan's last opposition has surrendered. We pray again, may God save His people.

I have been asked what I expect to accomplish. I am not out to "win" any argument. I am a Seventh-day Adventist minister whose work is to preach the truth and combat error. The Bible is mostly a record of the protest of God's witnesses against the prevailing sins of the church, and also of their apparent failure. Practically all protesters sealed their testimony with their blood, and the church went on until God intervened. All Paul hoped was that he might "save some." (1 Corinthians 9:22). Practically all the apostles died martyrs, and Christ they hanged on a tree. It took forty years before the destruction came. But when God intervened He did thorough work.

This denomination needs to go back to the instruction given in 1888, which was scorned. We need a reform in organization that will not permit a few men to direct every move made anywhere in the world. We need a reform that will not permit a few men to handle finances as is now being done. We need a reform that will not permit men to spend millions on institutions not authorized by the vote of the constituency, while mission fields are suffering for want of the barest necessities. We need a change in the emphasis that is given to promotion, finances and statistics. We need to restore the Sabbath School to its rightful place in the work of God. We need to put a stop to the entertainments and suppers that are creeping in under the guise of raising money for good purposes. We need to put a stop to the weekly announcements in church that are merely disguised advertisements. This list could be greatly enlarged.

But all these, while important, are after all only minor things. We need a reformation and revival most of all. If our leaders will not lead in this, "then shall there enlargement and deliverance arise to the Jews from another place." (Esther 4:14). I am of good cheer, praying for the peace of Israel.

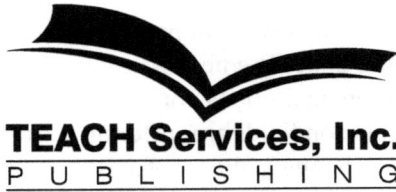

www.ingramcontent.com/pod-product-compliance
Lightning Source LLC
Chambersburg PA
CBHW070335090426
42733CB00012B/2483